GREAT RAILWAY PHOTOGRAPHS BY
ERIC TREACY

GREAT RAILWAY PHOTOGRAPHS BY

ERIC TREACY

Compiled by
G. FREEMAN ALLEN

General Editor
P. B. WHITEHOUSE ARPS

Introduction
DR J. A. COILEY

ℬℬ Bounty
Books

First published in Great Britain in 1982 by
David & Charles (Publishers) Limited
under the title *Eric Treacy Railway Photographer*

This edition published in 1997 by Chancellor Press,
an imprint of Bounty Books,
a division of Octopus Publishing Group Ltd
2–4 Heron Quays, London E14 4JP

Reprinted 1999, 2000, 2004 (twice)

ISBN 0 7537 0872 8

Printed in Hong Kong

Acknowledgement
The publisher is indebted to Ian Allen Ltd for permission
to quote from *Steam Up* and other titles in the introduction
by Dr J. A. Coiley

CONTENTS

FOREWORD

Shortly before he retired as Bishop of Wakefield Eric Treacy wrote to me to ask if I would be prepared, at his death, to take into my keeping all his photographic negatives of both film and plate – a great privilege and a task which I have gladly undertaken.

Tribute has been paid to Eric Treacy in many ways by many people. My intention – one I am sure shared by all his other railway friends – is to acknowledge our indebtedness to him as a photographer of railways, an enthusiast for railways, and as a true 'Steam Christian' with all that that term implies. The problem was how to do it properly. In the event I chose two friends, each of whom was connected with Eric Treacy over many years and who knew him well but in slightly differing spheres. John Coiley, the Keeper of the National Railway Museum at York, and Geoffrey Freeman Allen, well-known railway journalist and author, and son of that intrepid recorder of locomotive performance Cecil J. Allen. Since its completion Eric Treacy was so much part of the National Railway Museum and all it encompasses; it was a very important part of the later years of his life. His relationship with Geoffrey Allen was close over many years when they worked together in the publication of his pictures and books. In one way or another the three of us have spent many hundreds of pleasurable hours discussing the why and the wherefore, going through literally thousands of prints and negatives and finally whittling them down to the selection shown here.

Over the years numbers of Eric Treacy's pictures have appeared to delight those who have turned the pages of the railway press and the books which he carefully put together himself. It has not been our intention that these pictures should be kept out of this volume – far from it, for this is a tribute to his life's work. The final selection and the captioning of the pictures has been a somewhat daunting task, as few prints and even fewer negatives could have their subjects fully identified immediately due to lack of information because most of it had been kept in Eric Treacy's head!

Finally, we would like to thank May Treacy for all she did to encourage her man in his hobby – it has given more than pleasure to countless numbers.

P. B. WHITEHOUSE
Birmingham 1982

Class A3 Pacific No 60051 Blink Bonny had just returned from six post-war years on the GC main line to a brief spell at Copley Hill in 1955–7 before moving on to the NER when it was photographed rounding the bend past the Leeds shed with the up 'Yorkshire Pullman'.

Overleaf:
In the late 1930s a Skipton-based compound 4-4-0, No 1192, heads a lightweight restaurant car express out of Preston to the south.

7

INTRODUCTION

'I suppose every photographer has a vision of his ideal picture . . . so far, I haven't got it and I don't suppose I ever shall. I am aiming for something more than a picture – perhaps it is that I am wanting to do with my camera what I could only do with a box of water colours. It is I think, to catch that indefinable spell of the railway: to make visual something that can only be felt. Whatever it is I suppose I shall search for it all my life: this book is a record of my searchings.'

ERIC TREACY
'Steam Up' *1949*

It is a privilege to have been invited to write this introduction to a pictorial tribute to Eric Treacy, railway photographer and enthusiast extraordinary. This book contains a selection of some of his best photographs. As such it also serves to afford a unique opportunity on behalf of all his friends to express their appreciation of the enjoyment his pictures did indeed provide and for the pleasure his company provided those of us fortunate enough to have met him.

Although some of the photographs have been published before, they have not been seen for many years, possibly a generation ago. Moreover, it is the first time they have been included in one book and the selection made by those other than the photographer. In the hope that this volume will be read by some not as familiar with the railway photographs of Eric Treacy as are his friends and admirers I hope a few words about his life as a railway photographer and enthusiast will be helpful.

The photography of railways was a hobby for Eric Treacy. It provided a peaceful relaxation from his work in the Church where he rose to high office. He was born in 1907 but it was not until 1932 that he became a deacon in the Church of England at Liverpool. He married in the same year. From 1936 to 1940 he was Vicar of Edge Hill, Liverpool. After distinguished war service as Chaplain to the Forces for which he was awarded the MBE, he was made Rector of Keighley in 1945. From 1949 to 1961 he was Archdeacon of Pontefract, a post held until 1968 when he was appointed Bishop of Wakefield. This demanding position he held until his retirement in 1976 when he and his wife moved to live near Keswick in the shadow of Skiddaw.

Unlike most railway photographers Eric Treacy was first a photographer. Early in the 1930s when he was running a large boys' club in Liverpool he looked for some absorbing relaxation in the little spare time he had available. Organised activities such as games,

An evening scene at Edinburgh (Waverley) station with a B1 class 4-6-0 waiting to leave with a Thornton train.

11

rugby football in particular which he had enjoyed hitherto, were out of the question due to the time involved. Golf could not be entertained due to cost and time. He had however always been interested in the increasingly popular recreation of photography which appeared to fit in with the demands of his social work. Although there are somewhat conflicting accounts of what kind of camera he used for his first photograph, he declares that it all really started when he staked everything on the purchase of the then relatively new and small 35mm Leica camera, a step he says he never regretted. Having acquired a serious camera he looked to put it to serious use. Although photography was to be his relaxation he was resolute from the outset this was to be no excuse for a casual approach or lack of purpose. He was determined that he was not going to collect random snapshots of little use or interest in years to come.

Living and working in Merseyside in the 1930s meant that there was no lack of suitable subjects for a thoughtful photographer – the river, shipping, people of all nationalities going about their work, buildings old and new. Nevertheless he considered the matter carefully and while still reflecting had occasion to meet a friend at Lime Street station, Liverpool. On seeing the smoke, steam, light and shade and steam locomotives of all shapes and sizes, he knew immediately that he would attempt to capture the atmosphere of the steam railway. He conceded that it was a scene which could be better captured by a painter but nevertheless he would try to succeed 'through the lens of a camera'.

The important decision had been taken. Eric Treacy was going to photograph railways. Although unfortunately few if any of those early pictures with the Leica appear to have survived it is evident that his photography progressed, and by the mid-1930s his work was becoming known among railway enthusiasts, especially readers of *The Railway Magazine*. This publication of his earliest pictures was typical of the man – his wish to communicate to others his enthusiasm for photography and railways. One means of doing this was to submit prints to newspapers and journals known to publish pictures of railways. His first published photograph is the only one now known to be taken with that first Leica and was reproduced in the *Liverpool Post* showing a Royal Scot locomotive leaving Lime Street station with an express for London. When he used this again in 1948 he confessed that it was not his best picture but one can immediately understand why it was published. It displays a striking use of light and shade. The train dominates the picture but is cleverly framed by the massive arch of the station roof in the background.

In 1935 he became a member of the Railway Photographic Society a select group of serious photographers whose guiding light for 54 years was Maurice Earley, now elder statesman of railway photographers in this country. While Eric Treacy acknowledges on a number of occasions the help he received from RPS members he also remarks how similar was the work of the leading railway photographers. It appeared to be aimed, successfully, at producing a flaw-less portrait of a train. In doing this they very often missed the 'atmosphere', although he recognises there were many exceptions. He later admitted after the publication of his first booklet of pictures that much of his work in the 1930s suffered from a stylised approach with similar viewpoints and lighting. Fortunately however as his pictures show, that period also produced some of his very best work.

By the late 1930s it is already possible to examine some of the features that made an Eric Treacy photograph almost instantly re-cognisable, at that time in particular. A combination of streaks of romantic and artistic talent gave him an eye for composition in a suitable location. Partly by force of circumstances but partly, I sus-pect, by careful selection he took his pictures where the train was moving slowly and working hard, for example, leaving stations, climbing steep banks such as those out of Lime Street station or at Shap on the London to Glasgow main line. In this way not only did his trains look as if they were in action but his photographic task was rendered easier. He did not need such a fast shutter speed to freeze movement of the train and he could stop down the lens so giving a greater depth of focus or sharpness to the image. On other occasions the cooler air of northern climes may have revealed steam with more clarity than in the milder weather of the south of England where by chance most of the other railway photographers of the 1930s lived. Furthermore, most of the southern lines were more easily graded so that locomotives moved faster with less visible effort. At the same time it was only during the 1930s that colour sensitive emulsions for plates and films became available. Without these it was extremely difficult to render steam and clouds at all – only black smoke showing readily on colour-blind materials. While photo-graphers faced with these difficulties could have photographed trains leaving stations this required permits and special dispensations which were perhaps less readily available in the metropolis or the busier main lines of the south. Whatever the explanation, by the late 1930s Eric Treacy's pictures were well established in the magazines. They possessed high quality – well printed with sharp images to assist block making, good composition without extraneous huts or tele-graph poles, but using signals or men such as shunters and permanent way lengthmen to set off or balance the main subject, the steam engine at work whether shunting or at speed with an express.

While suitable colourful subjects may have abounded in those days, time did not. The demands of his work were such that his opportunities for photography were limited to 15 minutes in the morning and a similar period in the evening, provided the weather co-operated. Further opportunities arose during annual holidays which he and his wife invariably took in the Lake District. Although he was sometimes able to borrow a car they mostly went by train and he would take his bicycle in the guard's van. Needless to say they stayed within pedalling distance of the West Coast main line from

London to Glasgow where it climbs over the edge of the Lake District hills at Shap. Nevertheless the journeys to the lineside must have been hard work under a summer sun with a reflex camera perhaps weighing as much as 4½lb strapped to the handlebars (the Leica had been abandoned because of the small margin of error with exposure and processing techniques). In this way his Merseyside shots were augmented on Shap bank, at Penrith or Tebay stations and elsewhere in the area. Although he writes of using maps and planning, the time taken to find suitable locations and then in reaching them again, must have been great. In addition allowing for the vagaries of the weather and problems with the equipment, such as plagues of pinholes in the emulsion of his plates, the results of his efforts are remarkable. His best pictures of this 1937 – 39 period at Shap and elsewhere in the north west remain some of his finest of the steam locomotive in action. Not only are they technically first class but they convey the atmosphere of the occasion – man and machine at work in both industrial grime and gloom (who else but Eric Treacy would have ventured into the depths of the cutting between Lime Street and Edge Hill?) and wild rural settings. Furthermore they now have an important archive value depicting as they do something of the grand finale of the steam railway epoch with streamlined trains of blue and silver or maroon and gold, an era of a few short summers.

While his photographic experience was growing with his morning and evening lineside sessions other developments were taking place which were to have far reaching effects. His parish of Edge Hill encompassed a large locomotive depot which provided locomotives not only for the London expresses but many other duties in and about Liverpool. Through his work in the Church Eric Treacy came to know many of the men who worked on the locomotives as well as signalmen who regulated the trains through the parish and many of the army of permanent way men who maintained the running lines. With his warm and helpful nature it is not surprising that he soon found these men interested in his hobby. Help was often forthcoming with the result that his limited time at the lineside was put to best use. Increasingly he came to know the railway as a whole and its way of life. His appreciation of this wider aspect of the railway begins at this time to show in some of his photographs where shunters and permanent way staff help balance and composition in his pictures. At that time this was in marked contrast to the work of most other railway photographers who tended to see such incursions as distracting. On some occasions, perhaps on hot summer days when steam was absent, help would take the form of smoke by arrangement – a shovelful of coal at just the right time can make all the difference to a picture even if the hard headed expert regards it as a sign of inefficiency and bad firing.

At about this time his appreciation of the railway scene was further developed by his first footplate rides, from Liverpool to Crewe. Besides the enjoyment of these rides, he gained an insight into the

14

hard work, responsibility and team spirit involved in driving and especially firing a steam locomotive at the head of a heavy express. This experience undoubtedly helped his railway photography both directly and indirectly. While it may have left him with a few permanent marks as witness to how physically hard such rides can be on a locomotive in poor condition, it has left us with some splendid pictures of the driver's view ahead and work on the footplate. Before making these rides he would often photograph the preparation of the locomotive and related shed scenes and has left us with many striking interior studies of light and shade and plenty of atmosphere.

By the outbreak of the second world war, Eric Treacy had in this way become an established railway photographer who knew much about railway operation and the men of the railway. In 1940 he volunteered for the army and had little opportunity for railway photography until 1945. He does admit however to a little photography from time to time although it is now difficult to identify most such pictures with any certainty. One of the Royal Scot has been published many times and eventually dated as March 1942. He has subsequently admitted that it was taken during a wartime leave when he and his wife spent the day walking near Shap. Due to a miscalculation over lunch he had to run the last two miles to the lineside, only to find the train held halfway up the bank by signals. The picture of the subsequent restart with 16 carriages behind the Duchess locomotive is one of his best known pictures and deservedly so as it is one of his finest – he considered his best – on Shap.

In 1945 after leaving the Army he moved as Rector to Keighley in the then West Riding of Yorkshire. Here the railway scene was very different from Merseyside. He soon found however that many of the same ingredients for picture making were close at hand, industrial scenes, big city stations and Anglo-Scottish expresses, only this time they were on the old Midland Railway route over the Pennines by the Settle & Carlisle line – the 'Long Drag'. If time allowed, Shap itself was still only two hours away by car. He soon settled back into the ways of visiting these lineside locations as often as he could. Although trains on the Long Drag were less frequent than on the line over Shap, the locations were superb and offered more variation beneath the peaks of Pen-y-Ghent, Ingleborough or the viaducts at Ribblehead, Dent Head or Arten Gill, the tunnel at Blea Moor and finally the bleak summit of Ais Gill beneath Wild Boar Fell.

Besides his move to new locations, new opportunities were arising for the publication of his pictures. In 1946 a series of booklets was launched under the title *My Best Railway Photographs*. Number one in the LMS series was by Canon E. Treacy. This was very well received and endorsed his pre-war reputation. More of his pictures were now published in the monthly journals and *The Railway Magazine* was joined by *Trains Illustrated*. His pictures also served to illustrate an increasing number of books on railway matters in general. More special pictorial booklets followed and in 1949 his

15

first major work *Steam Up* was published. In this book, which many
regard as his best, he writes about his photography and his interest
in railways. From this and his introductions to the eight essentially
pictorial albums which followed over the years we also learn at first
hand of his love for the steam locomotive and the admiration and
respect for those who serve on the railways.

From *Steam Up* in 1949 until his death in 1978, Eric Treacy
published eight more volumes, the last, with George Heiron, not
appearing until 1979. During this period despite his increasingly
responsible duties in the Church, he was established without doubt
as the country's best known railway photographer and a leading
railway enthusiast and preservationist. Although he retired from his
bishopric in 1976 he continued taking railway pictures although by
now he was only able to find diesels, electrics or preserved steam. He
also experimented in colour. He died on 13 May 1978 at Appleby
station, on the Settle & Carlisle line he knew and loved so well, while
photographing *Evening Star*, one of his favourite locomotives, working a special train.

We are fortunate in making any assessment of his standing as a
photographer and railway enthusiast in that we have much of his
own revealing writing on the matter as well as his pictures. And so
we find him explaining the reason for his books in a typically modest
fashion. 'I make no pretension to expert knowledge about the works
of a steam locomotive nor the workings of a railway. My approach
is emotional rather than scientific. I love the railway – its smells, its
noises and its atmosphere, and I have a great regard for railwaymen.
I hope in this book (*Steam Up*) I may manage to communicate
something of my enthusiasm and something of the aesthetic beauty
which is to be found in the realm of the steam engine.'

These books provide many new clues to understanding how his
approach to railway photography led to such good pictures and how
he derived such enthusiasm for railways. In the previous quotation
he might have added something about the feeling of romance as well
as emotion. Only then is one able to begin to appreciate the spell of
the railway. He defines spell as '. . . a form of magic – an abstract'.
He writes at length about what the spell means to him.

'The Spell of the Railway is made up of so many things which
through the years have imprinted themselves on one's memory. Like
Wordsworth's Daffodils

> they flash upon that inward eye . . .
> then my heart with pleasure fills.

For me the spell began with those holiday journeys from Liverpool
to Penrith with the sight of the first stone wall between Carnforth
and Oxenholme; the distant Lakeland hills as the train began to
climb up to Shap – that lovely but sometimes sombre cutting at
Dillicar; then the slogging climb to Shap summit, what time the
engine's beat became indignantly emphatic; and the grazing sheep in

16

the fell fled to quieter pastures. A glimpse, perhaps, into that lonely one-man box at Scout Green – other glimpses into farm yards in which man and beast seemed to be momentarily transfixed.'

'The spell – it's the friendly noise of shunting during the long and wakeful hours of the night; and it is the noise of coal being broken in the tender as the engine awaits its job. It's the fussy little "Cauliflower" making its shaky way from Penrith to Keswick and it's the gleaming monster bringing its 500 tons into King's Cross. It's the sight of signal lights winking and gleaming on a winter's evening; it's the orange light of the fire reflected on the billowing steam of the engine at night. It's the deafening noise of an engine blowing off in a station; it's the sound of carriage doors being slammed; it's the noise of milk churns being trundled, of eerie whistles in the night, of a signal bell tinkling in a nearby box, of the heavy thud of a signal lever being operated . . .'

These are the expressions of a sensitive and observant man. They suggest for the spell to be totally effective the victim must be receptive, the eyes and ears open or as he says '. . . seeing, smelling, hearing – thus come our memories and impressions: thus is the spell created and thus maintained'.

Writing in 1949 he says '. . . It is the incentive of obtaining one day a picture which will express that ideal picture which is the motive of our work'. He must have been very close with some of his pictures. In their lighting composition, subject matter scores highly as does the imagination and technical competence of the photographer. On reflection however I think I would take issue with his assertion that there is only one ideal picture. Perhaps only one for each location but as we have already seen the variety is almost endless: main-line express, busy station, engine shed interior, view from the footplate. I suspect that Eric Treacy really thought this too and this was another reason why he photographed so widely and for nearly 50 years.

17

This variety of his high quality photography is perhaps what makes a volume of his pictures so memorable. The writing of Eric Treacy in his essentially pictorial books also varied widely from his surprise at how well the previous book sold (this from one of his earliest booklets) through several declamations that the present volume was his last, to his undying love for the steam locomotive. From time to time he would however pronounce on his attitudes to railway photography. While his views remained remarkably consistent over the 50 years or so he practised the art, he strangely or perhaps shrewdly never revealed all his secrets at one time. Thus we find that although he endorsed the familiar view that an expert will take a very good picture with a simple camera he made clear that it was obviously nonsense to expect to obtain a sharp picture of an express travelling at 80mph using a camera with a shutter speed no faster than 1/50 second. In other words the camera must be understood completely and not asked to undertake tasks for which it was not designed. He also held decided views on the impossibility of buying your way into good photography by using the most expensive equipment available. He does however admit to having succumbed to the temptation 'to exchange one perfectly good lens for another'.

Although he does not comment at length anywhere about the technical details of his photography he mentions that in addition to the original Leica he used two plate cameras, (a Soho ¼ plate reflex with a Cooke Aviar 7in lens and a Zeiss Contessa Press 9 × 12cm with a Zeiss Tessar 7in lens) and two roll-film cameras (a Zeiss Super Ikonta 3¼in × 2¼in fitted with a Zeiss Tessar lens and a 2¼in sq twin lens Rolleiflex). Some of his last pictures were taken with one or more modern press-type cameras of Japanese origin and fitted with roll film backs. Emulsions varied from Agfa Isopan (developed in Pyro-Metol) and Kodak P.1200 (developed in Johnson's Fine Grain developer) to Ilford HP3 (developed in Merito-Metol) and latterly Kodak Tri-X (developed in D76). Typical exposures were pre-war 1/1000 sec at f/6.3 with the Zeiss Tessar and Kodak P.1200 for a train moving at about 40mph. For really fast trains he would use a shutter speed of 1/2000 second when some distortion of the front of the train was just discernible due to the action of the focal plane shutter.

When writing about the cameras he used he also confesses to changes of mind over the suitability of camera type for the job. He went from pre-war plate camera to film and back to the same plate camera in the 1950s before abandoning plates entirely for roll film from about 1960 onwards. That he suffered such doubts should be encouragement to others who have suffered from similar agonies of indecision over equipment. That his picture quality never wavered during these technical reappraisals is a further measure of his mastery of the art.

Although he refers to having a camera with him all the time 'just in case' and to taking pictures when the opportunity arose, for example, while changing trains, he always had in his mind the various types of picture he sought. There was no question of casual snap-shots. This was a result of his very definite strictures that the only way to good pictures was by planning. In his very first (1946) booklet of his own photographs he says '. . . certain rules govern my photo-graphic efforts and they are these: (1) To photograph only in proper lighting conditions. From the beginning of November to the begin-ning of March I put my cameras away and attempt no photography. At this time of the year the light is too weak to obtain results. Normally I photograph only in sunlight; it is very rarely and for some special reason that I have operated in dull weather and I have never been satisfied with the results. (2) To use imagination in composing my pictures. Whenever I go on a train journey I am on the look-out for good positions alongside the line for future photo-graphic reference, carefully noting the position of the sun to decide at what time of day it will be suitable for the purpose. I have by me a large number of places which I hope to visit some day. The ¾ view of a train is the most obvious and for that reason is often rather tedious. Admittedly, there are not many ways of taking a moving train but it is worth making bold experiments. Ideally one should have plenty of time to choose one's view point otherwise trees may be found growing out of the boiler or telegraph poles sprouting out of the chimney. It should be possible to place the train in relation to the landscape so that the result is a picture rather than a mere photographic record. (3) To standardise plates and developers so that I know just how the emulsion will behave in a variety of circumstances.'

These then were some of the views and methods of the leading railway photographer of his time. From the evidence of his pictures he adhered to these guidelines throughout. After steam on British Railways ceased in August 1968 he turned more and more to diesels, electrics and preserved steam. He experimented with colour tran-sparencies. His interest in railways and photography was such that he was still prepared to spend some of his increasingly precious spare time photographing modern traction. While he found this satisfying if somehow the picture conveyed railway atmosphere, it was hard work since even Eric Treacy found it almost impossible to inject life into diesels and electrics. He relied on new locomotives or routings and new trains for interest, but most of all setting this new machinery in the station, junctions and countryside locations he had come to know so well in days of steam. Of diesels he said little but of Deltics, the successors to the sleek streamlined Pacifics on the East Coast main line, he said 'if you have to have diesel-electric locomotives then a Deltic is about the best you can get – but what a contrast'. During these latter days of his hobby there is some evidence that he was prepared to photograph on occasions without sun. While this may have been due in some measure to improvements in materials and equipment it is more likely that time for photography was becoming more difficult to find. As was to be expected these pictures were very good if lacking a little in the dramatic quality that comes only with the interplay of light and shade.

It was during this period that he became even more widely known – the Bishop who for his entry in *Who's Who* gave his hobby as 'pottering about locomotive sheds'. The Railway Bishop had been created. During these years as Bishop of Wakefield he relates that many happy things happened to him in connection with railway events which gave him great pleasure. A privately-owned ex LMS Class 5 4-6-0 steam locomotive was named *Eric Treacy* by the Bishop of Birmingham. He was invited to open the preserved Lakeside & Haverthwaite Railway by Lake Windermere. And finally he was invited to become President of the Keighley & Worth Valley Railway in the heart of the country he had known so well when working in Keighley and later Halifax. He was also the President of the Birmingham Railway Museum at Tyseley. On retirement he was able to visit the new National Railway Museum at York on a number of occasions and presented numbers of his books and paintings to the museum. He was an ardent supporter of the Museum and was delighted when he was appointed the nominee of the Secretary of State for the Council of the Friends of the National Railway Museum established in 1977.

In these and similar ways he received rich recognition during his life-time for the pleasure and enthusiasm he had conveyed to many with his love of railways. After his death further handsome tributes were paid him. British Rail ran two steam hauled special trains over the Settle & Carlisle line to Appleby station where a memorial service was held and a memorial plaque unveiled. The Friends of the National Railway Museum have established with assistance from British Rail and the Steam Locomotive Operators Association an annual photographic competition to be known as the 'Bishop Treacy Photographic Competition' with special awards to encourage young photographers. Finally, an electric locomotive from the West Coast main line over Shap was named *Bishop Treacy* by Mrs Treacy at Penrith in May 1979.

Eric Treacy left his own unique and enduring memorial – his photographs. As long as trains are photographed Eric Treacy will be remembered. He and his work will be remembered by the occasional photographer on the slopes of Shap or Beattock and by the hundreds following for a few years yet, the last preserved steam engines on the main line from Ribblehead to Ais Gill and back again and even those who pursue the steam engine in the remoter parts of Africa, Asia or the Americas. In years to come when perhaps in Britain there are no longer big hills for the steam engines to climb on the main-line, future generations will be able to admire his pictures in volumes such as this. They should be grateful for the fruits of a pastime of a truly remarkable man who loved people, life and steam engines.

York shed in the early autumn of 1967. The engine is No 7029 Clun Castle, temporarily housed there while running clearance trials before the series of trains it hauled over the Eastern Region later that year. Name and number plates were removed for security reasons.

20

J. A. COILEY
Knaresborough, 1982

SCOTS ON MERSEYSIDE

I first experienced Eric Treacy's art through his pre-war shots of the original parallel-boiler Royal Scots in and around Liverpool. 'Experience' is the word. I can still vividly remember how, as a schoolboy, I could almost feel the engines' presence as they leaped at me from the superbly crisp whole-plate prints he sent my father, it was a sensation I had never got from anyone else's photographs, professional or amateur, in the bulging files of CJA.

By the time Eric first aimed his camera at them the Scots were both better looking and better performers than when they were born. Take looks first. The 1931–2 fitment of all 70 engines with full-size smoke deflectors had added much-needed visual strength at the front end. The chimney was no longer such a puny mis-match for a fattish dome and the extra smokebox girth of an already chubby boiler, and the deflectors added a sense of powerful thrust which was intensified by Eric's dramatic ground-level angle on Scots cleaving the murk of the Lime Street tunnels or leaning to the Edge Hill curve. Thank heaven none of the grotesque smokebox-top contraptions which the LMS tried on the engines in 1929–31 to counteract a drifting exhaust nuisance were satisfactory, though it took a catastrophic 1931 cross-over derailment at Leighton Buzzard, in which obscurity of the driver's vision of cautionary signals was said to have been a factor, to persuade the LMS to adopt full-size, Continental-style deflectors. This was strongly urged in the ensuing Ministry Inspector's report.

The indifferent initial work of the Scots was probably inevitable considering the haste in which they were conceived. After the LMS 1926 loan of a GW Castle to help settle the wrangles over future locomotive building policy had discredited Derby's Midland-school dogmatists, Fowler's compound Pacific draft had been pigeon-holed, and the North British Locomotive Co had been handed an urgent order to design and build a 4-6-0 with Castle affinities. The Glasgow firm had the detail plans sketched, metal cut and no fewer than 50 engines on the road within 12 months.

You never knew what to expect from a Scot in their early years. As one lineside observer at Rugeley put it in a letter to my father, a Scot would purr by with 13 on one day and the next another of the class with only 11 or 12 in tow could be heard shouting from afar, then seen to be ejecting a firestorm of cinders as it laboured into view. To some drivers they were beauties, to others barely the equal of an LNW Claughton or Prince of Wales in good nick. Some Scot engine-crews were getting through nine tons of coal on the Euston-

The classic Treacy Edge Hill cutting location. A pre Second World War photograph of an up express climbing from Liverpool (Lime Street) station headed by Royal Scot class 4-6-0 No 6130 The West Yorkshire Regiment.

23

Carlisle run, whereas little more than five had been the norm on the LNW 4-6-0 types.

The reason for that extravagance was soon traced to flawed design in the heads of the piston valves, which let a great deal of steam go straight from boiler to exhaust without doing a scrap of work. That was rectified on the whole class early in the 1930s. At the same time West Coast enginemen got the hang of driving and firing the Scots for best effect, and the engines began to show pace on light loads as well as comfortable command of 500-ton trains south of Crewe.

Some of highest speeds by the Scots were recorded in September 1933, when the then Humber-Hillman-Commer motor company chartered some lavish specials to convey London guests to and from their plant at Coventry. Evidently determined that road transport should not dominate the prestigious travellers' day, the LMS not only set tight schedules for the specials but apparently had given drivers a covert nod to do better if they could. On No 6129 *Comet* (renamed *The Scottish Horse* in 1935 when all the early Scot names commemorating early 19th century locomotives were scrapped in favour of regiments) Driver Marchant took the tip and ran his seven-coach, 212-ton train over the 94 miles from Coventry to Euston in 79 minutes, and that included a dead stand for signals on Camden bank. He had *Comet* up to 90mph before Weedon, 92 at Castlethorpe, 90 again at Kings Langley and a culminating 91½ at Wembley. Throughout the 69¾ miles from Welton to Willesden he averaged just over 85mph.

With a heavier load of 11, grossing 334 tons, and the same engine, Driver J. Jones was only a minute and half behind his colleague's time as far as Willesden, having averaged 80.8mph to that point from Welton, but then he got a much worse clobbering from signal checks. In the reverse direction, again with *Comet*, the Camden firebrand of the day, Laurie Earl, took the palm. He had the same 11-car rake of 334 tons into Coventry in just over 87 minutes despite a loss of two minutes to signal checks at Tring and without exceeding 85mph. But then Earl never reckoned the Scots to be as nippy as Patriots and was always sceptical of claims that Scots had been coaxed above 90mph.

In the mid-1930s, of course, Stanier's first Pacifics robbed the original Scots of the prime West Coast jobs, but the 4-6-0s still had a chance to shine on the Euston-Manchester expresses and clung to a share of the Liverpool work. Though their proudest days were to come with taper-boiler building, the Euston-Coventry sprints earned a 1933 tribute from CJA that 'it is doubtful if Great Britain has ever witnessed finer exploits of locomotive speed than these, given due consideration of the undulating character of the road'.

The crimson-and-cream livery of the coaching stock, standardised in 1949 but discarded for all-maroon in 1957, dates this Lime Street scene in the mid-1950s. One of Camden shed's rebuilt, taper-boiler Scots, No 46144 *Honourable Artillery Company*, gets a grip of a Euston train.

A Crewe-based Scot, No 6126 *Royal Army Service Corps*, winds a Liverpool-West of England train past Edge Hill. It is probably the 10.45 off Lime Street, with through GWR coach to Penzance immediately behind the tender.

Facing page:
The electrified West Coast main line: No 87.005, the most modern type of BR electric Bo-Bo, at speed with a rake of Mk II coaching stock.

Another Liverpool–Euston express of the late 1930s is headed past Wavertree by No 6142, originally *Lion*, but renamed *The York & Lancaster Regiment* in 1936. Eric Treacy's notes on the reverse of the print advise that the photograph was taken with his 9 × 12 Zeiss Contessa Process, with a Zeiss Tessar 7in lens, and that the exposure was 1/1000 at f5.6.

Reproduced in the September 1937 Railway Magazine, *this picture was most likely taken in the summer of 1936. It is a memory of the pre-war 'Sunny South Express', seen at Wavertree. Royal Scot 4-6-0 No 6155* The Lancer *is setting out with the three coaches from Liverpool to Eastbourne, which will be amalgamated at Crewe with a four-coach Manchester–Eastbourne section including restaurant car. Sister engine No 6112* Sherwood Forester *stands on the adjoining track.*

Facing page:
Morning glory: in the late 1930s No 6143 The South Staffordshire Regiment, *one of Edge Hill's allocation of Royal Scots, rounds Edge Hill curve with the 10.10 am Liverpool Lime Street–Euston 'Merseyside Express'. This was the opening picture in Eric Treacy's first book of photos, Steam Up.*

A PARADE OF PATRIOTS

*Another superb Patriot study at Edge Hill,
but this time early in the nationalisation
era, with the engine renumbered by BR but
the coaching stock still wearing LMS livery
and LMS roofboards. Edge Hill's No 45518*
Bradshaw *heads an express from Liverpool
to Birmingham. In time the unrebuilt
Patriots graduated to BR's lined-green
express passenger livery.*

Nominally only the last ten Patriots, built in 1934, were new engines. The LMS accounted the other 42 as rebuilds of ex-LNW four-cylinder Claughton 4-6-0s, whose greed for coal and fretting of motive power chiefs with heavy repair bills, no manner of tinkering with Caprotti valve gear, blastpipe modifications, piston valve adjustment or reboilering had managed to tame. In 1930, when Fowler was still in command at Derby, someone thought to marry the final, big Claughton boiler with a three-cylinder Royal Scot chassis. Hence the tag of 'Baby Scot' soon applied to the first two prototypes of 1930, though the LMS preferred the type to be known as the Patriot after it had adopted a suggestion that this name, borne by a Claughton which was the LNWR's mobile war memorial engine, be transferred to one of the prototypes.

Branding the Patriots as rebuilds may have kept the capital account within budget and satisfactorily deluded the shareholders, but it was almost total fiction. The first two engines did actually take over Claughton bogies and driving wheel centres, but the rest, boilers included, was brand-new. As for the 40 further alleged rebuilds, it is highly doubtful that any Claughton metal went into them at all, unless it had been melted down and re-forged.

One Camden driver of the 1930s at least revelled in the Patriots. That was fiery little Lawrie Earl. 'Grand engines, very light on coal', he once wrote of them. 'At times my fireman and I would experiment to see on how little coal we could bring the 8.30 from Manchester up to London. Once, with a six-coach train of 189 tons, I made up the fire myself; six times only was enough for the entire run, with plenty put in at a time, of course, but spread carefully over the grate. The last firing was at Blisworth, after which the fire wasn't touched again for 63 miles up to Euston. I always thought the Patriots had a better turn of speed than the Royal Scots, though I liked the Scots well enough.'

*An unidentified Patriot climbing out of
Liverpool past Edge Hill takes assistance
from one of Crewe North's Class 2P 4-4-0s
in the late 1930s. In those days no one
worried about marshalling a fixed-
wheelbase van between the engine and
coaches of an express train certain to travel
as fast as 70mph, if not higher.*

The LMS took its time over naming the Patriots and a few were still anonymous when they passed into BR's hands, but No 5527 Southport was among the first to be honoured, in 1937. Edge Hill-based in the late 1930s, it figures here in one of Eric Treacy's most striking Edge Hill shots, heading an express away from Liverpool.

This absolutely immaculate, red-liveried Patriot must have posed for Eric Treacy at Edge Hill depot in 1938, just before its naming that year as Bangor; No 5523's nameplate mounts are in position, but not the plates themselves.

THE STREAMLINER YEARS

The streamliner era opened for me on the still unforgettable Friday afternoon of 17 September 1935. I was on my last summer holiday vigil on New Barnet station footbridge before the start of the winter school term. It must have been almost teatime, because in those days the GN main line in the North London suburbs was a desert in the early afternoon, with only the 3 p.m. down to East Lincolnshire – still an Ivatt Atlantic job in 1935 as I recall – to rouse interest until the far-famed 'Scotch Goods', then K3 2-6-0 hauled because the V2 2-6-2's debut was still a year ahead, and the heavy 4 p.m. to the West Riding and Newcastle. Southbound, the only mid-afternoon event of consequence was the 'Yorkshire Pullman's' passage.

Strangely, I cannot remember my father having any inkling, even as late as September 1935, of the fruit ripening from the exploits of *Flying Scotsman* and *Papyrus* which he had timed in November 1934 and March 1935. And the lineside gossip channel in the mid-1930s was as a feeble smoke signal to a Time Division Multiplex system compared with the advance briefing available to any schoolboy 50 years later. So I was totally nonplussed when a repeated, ship siren-like call, but much more melodious, was borne on the wind from Hadley Wood, from the treeline of which there soon emerged a silver-grey UFO.

Silver Link was on her way up light engine from Doncaster works to Kings Cross to prepare for the following Friday's epic 'Silver Jubilee' demonstration to the press, by which time I was back at school. I can still hear the wail of her chime whistle that previous Friday afternoon as a proud driver drew the attention of every signalbox, station and bystander he could spot to his charge on the way up to town.

A family tie in North London gave Eric Treacy some opportunities to cover the GN main line in those four exciting pre-war streamliner years. His shot at that time of *Quicksilver* bursting from Oakleigh Park tunnel with the down 'Silver Jubilee' vividly recalls for me each weeknight's drama at New Barnet.

The curtain-raiser featured the unlikeliest performer, an LMS 'Jinty' 0-6-0 tank. Somehow those stumpy little engines resisted every attempt to displace them from the through North London services between Broad Street and the Hertfordshire suburbs with bigger and more suitable machines, such as the Fowler 2-6-2 tanks. So in the mid-1930s a 'Jinty' was still standard power even for the 5.7 p.m. Broad Street–Potters Bar, the 'Stockbrokers' Special', which was

35

Class K3 2-6-0 No 2428 emerges from Hadley Wood tunnel with an up brake-fitted freight in 1938.

uniquely – for a North London train – non-stop from Finsbury Park to New Barnet. Since a 'Jinty's' driving wheels were only 4ft 7in – 3in less than the diameter of a Class N7 0-6-2T wheels, and those GE tanks' rods flashed merrily enough when they were occasionally deployed on Kings Cross–Hatfield workings – the 5.7 was a pretty lively spectacle by the time its driver had grafted up to his best pace before shutting off in the vicinity of New Barnet South box.

Night after night, even in 1936 and 1937 as I remember, a substantial knot of the 5.7's City folk hung back from the New Barnet exit stairs when their train stopped. Instead they stood waiting for the distant explosion of stentorian exhaust as the 'Jubilee' emerged from Oakleigh Park tunnel, then thrilled with me as the A4's challenging outline rounded the bend into the Oakleigh Park–New Barnet straight and the air quivered to a furious three-cylinder crescendo. No one brought up in the era of Deltics and HST can possibly imagine the sensation of having an A4 storm on you full-throated at 70mph up a gradient where Pacifics had previously toiled no faster than 50mph at best.

An awe-inspiring second as the A4 pounded past, a shimmer of silver-grey coaches speckled with the red of Pullman-like table lamps, accompanied by a crisp tattoo of articulated bogie wheels, and it was all over. The grandstand made for the stairs. Then, as the 'Jubilee's' tail-lights disappeared in Hadley Woods, the slow line platform somersault starter dropped with a clang and the 5.7's 'Jinty' flexed its muscles for another tough little assignment – clearance of what was then the Hadley Wood bottleneck and evacuation of the Potters Bar down platform and on to the four track section beyond before the appearance of the 5.45 Kings Cross–Newcastle. Come to think of it, smart working of the 'Jinty' on that turn must have been fairly crucial to each weeknight's smooth exit of the peak provincial departures from Kings Cross.

No 4482 Golden Eagle was the first of five green-liveried A4s built in the 1936-7 winter for general East Coast main line express work and here heads the down 'Flying Scotsman' away from Finsbury Park. Garter blue was standardised for the entire class after the choice of that livery for the 1937 streamlined trains.

Facing page, top:
Class A4 No 2510 Quicksilver emerges from Oakleigh Park tunnel with the down 'Silver Jubilee', probably in the 1938 summer, as the engine is in Garter blue livery, which it received in December 1937. The speed of the streamliner up the bank to Potters Bar is suggested by the pronounced curve of the exhaust.

Facing page, bottom:
One of the five A4s originally assigned to the 1937 'Coronation' streamliner, No 4492 Dominion of New Zealand, passes Hadley Wood on what is probably a Cambridge running-in turn of Kings Cross shed in the late 1930s, since the first three vehicles are non-corridor stock of GNR 1908 pattern.

Class A1 4-6-2 No 2560 Pretty Polly, a Grantham-based Pacific from late 1928 until late 1942, clambers up the bank to Potters Bar with the 5.54 p.m. Kings Cross–Newcastle in the summer of 1938.

The down 'Yorkshire Pullman', the 4.45 p.m. from Kings Cross, passes Hadley Wood behind No 4900 Gannet in the summer of 1938, when this Pacific was shedded at Doncaster. The final shape of the A4's wheel casing was not agreed until the first A4 was well advanced in construction, when it was too late to produce detailed drawings: to secure the true aerofoil configuration Gresley insisted upon, works staff had to fix planks of wood to the half-finished No 2509's flanks and mark off on them a curve calculated from drawings of the R101 airship.

THE 'CROSS' IN THE FIFTIES

Preparing for the morning exodus at Kings Cross Top Shed: Class A4 Pacifics Nos 60010 Dominion of Canada *and 60014* Silver Link, *with Class K3 2-6-0 No 61852.*

Many of Eric Treacy's finest East Coast Pacific pictures were shot in the vicinity of Kings Cross in the mid-1950s, when determined action to stop the rot of the immediate post-war neglect of Pacifics through common-user employment was showing results. In the late 1940s the Eastern and North Eastern Region's struggle to revive a substantial quota of through locomotive workings between London and both the West Riding and Tyneside had overtaxed sheds which were pushed enough to keep war-weary engines in working order and up to the required performance standard on indifferent coal. Some of them, Kings Cross especially, were also losing the battle to keep skilled fitters from the clutches of a resurgent industry prepared to bid high wages for key labour. And in any event the overnight lodging turns which most of the through workings postulated were a bone of bitter contention with some of the enginemen's union branches affected, especially in the North-East.

So in 1951 Grantham was re-appointed a key engine-change point, with a stock of eight A3 Pacifics and 11 A1s. The Eastern Region's A4s were concentrated at Kings Cross, and both Kings Cross and Grantham then grasped the opportunity of the revised rosters to assign specific engines to a pair of nominated crews for coverage of the principal trains. At Kings Cross nine A4s were the exclusive property in each case of a couple of crews, among whom several drivers became inseparably associated with their engines – Simmons and Hoole with No 60007 *Sir Nigel Gresley*, for instance, Hailstone with No 60014 *Silver Link*, Tappin with No 60015 *Quicksilver* and Dines with No 60028 *Walter K. Whigham*. The benefit showed both in performance and in the carefully tended external appearance of the engines, in the latter case as the following pictures bear witness. As to reliability, in the 1952 summer the London–Edinburgh non-stop was only once crippled by an A4 failure, and that as the direct result of defective lubricant, not of any mechanical malfunction.

As the 1950s progressed the Kings Cross A4s were supplemented by A1s and A3s. By the autumn of 1957 there were no fewer than 42 Pacifics on the shed's allocation.

If the detail of No 60133's appearance – no name, no chimney capuchon, no crest on the tender – did not date this Kings Cross scene as 1949, then a glimpse of the gallery at No 10 platform's end should: not a camera to be seen. No 60133 was actually the first A1 to be named, in April 1950, when BR decided that it no longer needed to eschew naming as a concession to post-war austerity. No 60133 was a Grantham engine when this picture was taken.

The all-maroon train-set of the northbound 'Flying Scotsman' leaving Copenhagen Tunnel dates this picture around 1959, after the A4s had been completely fitted with double chimneys and when No 60015 Quicksilver was in all probability deputising for one of the GN Line's then very fallible Class 40 diesels and essaying exactly the same daily roster to Newcastle with the 'Scotsman' and back the same day with the 5 p.m. from Tyneside.

Class A4 No 60028 Walter K. Whigham emerges from Gasworks Tunnel with the northbound 'Yorkshire Pullman'.

The maroon-and-cream 'Norseman', headed by single-chimney A4 60026 Miles Beevor, passes No 60033 Seagull, one of the quartet built pre-war with a double chimney, coming off Kings Cross shed and waiting for a path down to the 'Cross' to take on the 'Elizabethan'. Both engines demonstrate how 'Top Shed' tested the loading gauge to the limit when they coaled an outgoing A4.

Overleaf:
The world record-breaker, No 60022 Mallard, pulls out with the 'Jubilee's' post-war substitute, the 'Tees-Tyne Pullman'. The fourth vehicle is the Hadrian Bar, specially created for the train's 1948 debut by a conversion at the Pullman Company's Preston Park works, Brighton, of a 1928-built third-class car, No 59. The down 'Tees-Tyne' was one of the first two GN main line trains to recover a 60mph timing after the war.

Class N2 0-6-2T No 69492 battles with the gradient past Kings Cross Goods with the empties of an overnight sleeper. Kings Cross shed never found any LNER tank type to outclass the N2 on this difficult job, which was a perennial worry to the local operators, especially in winter; the shed eventually concluded that the ideal horse for the job would have been one of the Western's eight-coupled tanks, but it never got its hands on any – and if it had there would probably have been clearance snags.

Steam suburban successor Mk I: the ten English Electric Class 23 1,100hp 'Baby Deltics' should have been the GN London Area's first diesel acquisitions in 1958, but because of various snags arrived a year late, and soon succumbed to chronic failures that had them withdrawn in May 1962 for thorough engine rebuilding. No D5901 emerges from Gasworks Tunnel with two quad sets of stock.

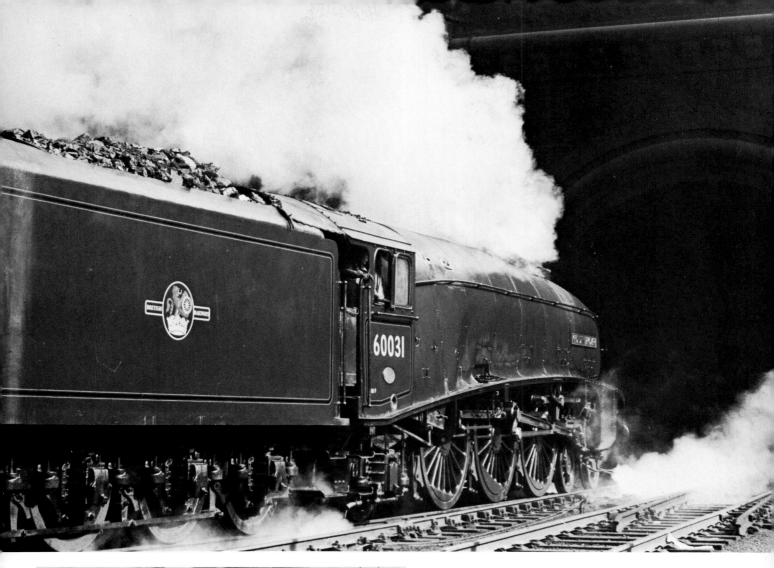

A4 No 60031 Golden Plover, *a Haymarket engine all its life apart from its final three years on the Glasgow–Aberdeen road from St Rollox, plunges into Gasworks Tunnel with the 'Elizabethan'* ...

... *and Kings Cross A4 No 60029 Woodcock emerges spectacularly on the north side.*

Overleaf:
The immaculate condition of Kings Cross A3 No 60055 Woolwinder, barking past the entrance to Kings Cross Goods Yard with the down 'White Rose', contrasts sharply with the filth of New England Class A2/3 No 60514 Chamossaire coming off Top Shed on the right, probably to work the 10.10 down, on which a New England engine then returned after bringing up the overnight 'Aberdonian' from Peterborough.

47

THE ROUTE OF THE 'IRISH MAIL'

Eric Treacy's capture of the 'Irish Mail' double-headed by a Class 2P 4-4-0 and a Royal Scot reproduced on pages 52/3 is another of the striking pre-war prints which immediately stamped him as a new dean of railway photography. The piloting of the Scot on this occasion seems to have been unusual, for though the 'Mails' of the late 1930s were not fast enough to achieve a throughout Dublin–London time equal to that offered by the LNWR at the start of the century, they normally confronted an unaided Scot with some of the heaviest loads set the class anywhere on the LMS. Day 'Irish Mail' logs of 1938 record rakes of 16 or even 17 coaches, grossing as much as 540 tons loaded, which the 4-6-0 hauled unchanged between Euston and Holyhead in each direction.

Since the postal vans were at one end of the formation and did station business en route, Scot drivers had to judge their braking quite finely to halt such a long train neatly within the platform length. On one of Cecil J. Allen's up trips Chester was overshot by the length of the postal vans: the gingerly set-back cost minutes which – CJA reported with ill-concealed distaste – seemed mainly sacrificed to ensure timely railing of the week's football pool entries from the area.

Considering its usual tonnage, the up day 'Mail' was no slouch by the standards of the late 1930s. Subtract the quite lengthy time allowed for station stops, and the Scot had to shift its 500 tons-plus over the 263.5 miles from Holyhead to Euston in 285 minutes, facing a final challenge of an 82-minute booking for the 82 miles from Rugby to London.

Princess Royal Pacifics were briefly applied to the 'Irish Mail', but Holyhead was one of the first sheds to get rejuvenated Scots when rebuilding of the class with taper boilers began in 1943. They monopolised the 'Mails' until 1954, when the first five Britannia Pacifics turned out with the 9 ton-coal capacity Type BR1D tender, Nos 70045-9, were assigned to Holyhead. A year earlier Nos 70030-4 had been allocated to Holyhead, but they were very smartly moved on to Longsight because their smaller BR1 tenders could not cope with the demands of the 'Irish Mail' turn.

Ex-Lancashire & Yorkshire 0-6-0 No 52230
potters about Bangor yard in the 1950s.

One of Stanier's least successful designs,
his Class 3 2-6-2 tank, though it was a
marginal improvement on its Fowler
predecessor, which one LMS motive power
man has damned as unable to supply
'enough heat to mash tea in a busy
refreshment room'. No 73 is ambling past
Bethesda Junction, Bangor, with a pre-war
Llandudno-Bangor local.

A Bangor-based Stanier 'Black Five' 4-6-0, No 5346, moves away from its home with a Chester stopping train on the eve of the last war. The prodigality of pre-war signalling is in evidence; the signalbox in the foreground could almost shout messages to its neighbour, visible to the left of the train's last coach.

The up day 'Irish Mail' climbs out of Holyhead past the port's shed soon after nationalisation. Rebuilt Scot No 46127 Old Contemptibles is still in black livery, but with BR's early LNWR-style lining, and naked of smoke deflectors; it was 1949 before the rebuilt engines began gradually to acquire them.

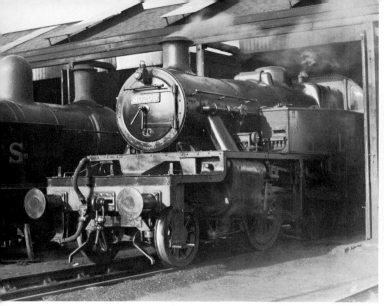

Another Stainer Class 3 2-6-2T, No 40209, in BR ownership; though it wears a Willesden shedplate it is posing at Llandudno Junction shed alongside an ex-Lancashire & Yorkshire 2-4-2T.

The up 'Irish Mail' of the late 1930s, double-headed by Class 2P 4-4-0 and Royal Scot 4-6-0 No 6112 Sherwood Forester, passes Bethesda Junction, Bangor.

THE 'LONG DRAG'S'
EXPRESS POWER

Eric Treacy's work on the Settle–Carlisle main line, the Long Drag, seems to have started more or less coincidentally with the drafting of Royal Scot 4-6-0s to the route's principal trains. They dominated the express passenger working over Ais Gill throughout the 1950s.

The Long Drag's six-coupled era had opened in 1928. Immediately after the Grouping the LMS had pitted an LNW Claughton 4-6-0 and an LNW inside-cylinder Prince of Wales 4-6-0 against the line's then staple four-coupled express passenger power, the Midland compounds and Class 3s, but was evidently unimpressed by the conclusions. By 1928–9, however, management had become intolerant of the cost of double-heading so many of the Long Drag's steadily heavier trains. With the availability of 50 new Royal Scot 4-6-0s on the Western Division, 25 of the latter's Claughtons were shifted to the Midland, eight to Kentish Town, twelve to Leeds Holbeck and five to Carlisle Durran Hill shed.

As was ever the way with such moves, the Western Division sheds happily assembled their most unloved delinquents for the transfer – and in a class as variable both in performance and mechanical resilience as the original Claughtons that must have produced a collection fit for the knacker's yard. Small wonder that it took Midland crews and shed staff, inherently antipathetic to any Crewe product, a matter of years, not months, to make anything of the engines. As late as the 1930–1 winter records show that Holbeck and Durran Hill not only had several of their Claughtons stopped for repairs more days than they were on work, but that Holbeck at least was frequently leaving almost half its Claughtons cold on shed, even when they were serviceable, and using other types instead. As the 1930s progressed, though, the Midland men got on terms with the Claughtons and ran some of them very competently on rosters that set the engines two Leeds–Carlisle return trips each weekday. O. S. Nock once timed one at up to 88mph on the descent from Blea Moor to Settle.

At the end of 1930 one of the first two Patriot 4-6-0 prototypes, the eventual No 5500 *Patriot*, was assigned to the Long Drag and so delighted the local enginemen that a number of the subsequent so-called rebuilds of this type were sent to Holbeck shed. That was the end of the original Claughtons' Leeds–Carlisle duty. Then in the mid-1930s came the Stanier three-cylinder Jubilees to share the most taxing jobs with the Patriots, and the 'Black Fives' to shoulder some of the lighter express turns, such as the 'Thames–Forth Express', which normally amounted only to five St Pancras–Edinburgh Waverley coaches between Leeds and Carlisle.

One of the outstanding climbs from Carlisle to Ais Gill summit stands to a Jubilee's credit. In October 1937 No 5660 *Rooke* was selected to probe the scope for acceleration on the LMS ex-Midland cross-country routes in a four-day, four-stage test with a nine-coach train of 302 tons from Bristol to Leeds, thence to Glasgow and then back the same way. Going north *Rooke* covered the 14 miles from Settle Junction to Blea Moor at an average of 51.4mph, with a minimum of 46mph, and fulfilled the 117-minute timing it had been set for the 113 miles from Leeds to Carlisle despite a discouraging sequence of engineering slacks.

On the return *Rooke* dismissed the 48.4 miles from Carlisle to Ais Gill summit in an astonishing 48 minutes 36 seconds, topping the climb at 46.5mph. A measure of the 4-6-0's phenomenal ascent is that it took seconds less over the 17.5 miles from Appleby to Ais Gill signalbox than the prototype Deltic – which, granted, was fronting 642 tons – when the diesel was being submitted to BR's efficiency test routines in the late 1950s (the outcome of which, of course, ignited the Eastern Region's campaign for a production series).

The progressively heavier loading of the Settle–Carlisle route's trains and the inflation of its traffic in the last war's early years made an infusion of higher power imperative. The reserve of pilots for double-heading was all but non-existent. Bridges were strengthened to admit Royal Scots to the route in 1941 and in the following year Stanier's first two Jubilee rebuilds with 250lb boilers, Nos 5735 and 5736, were posted to Holbeck. In 1943 they were exchanged for the unique No 6170 *British Legion*, the taper-boiler rebuild as a conventional locomotive of the ill-starred high-pressure boiler Royal Scot experiment No 6399 *Fury*, and the first of the taper-boiler Rebuilt Scots, No 6103. By the end of that year five of the Rebuilt Scots were based at Holbeck and their reign had begun.

Their rule was not seriously challenged until 1959, by which time Holbeck and the rest of the Leeds area had been made a North Eastern Region responsibility, when Britannia Pacifics Nos 70044 from the LMR and 70053/4 from Scotland, displaced by diesels, were moved to Holbeck. The Long Drag's brief Pacific age culminated in 1960 when East Coast Route dieselisation released Gresley Class A3 Pacifics, and after earlier experiments with Peppercorn A1s the NER moved six of its A3 allocation from Tyneside to Holbeck. According to the gossip of the day the East Coast Pacifics were second choice for the job; in the spring of that year the alternative of switching NER diesels to the LMR and releasing Stanier Pacifics for Long Drag duty had been seriously considered.

The bleakness of the Long Drag on the exposed Pennine moorlands is only too apparent in this quartet of Treacy photographs depicting the variety of motive power which the Midland route to Scotland saw in the closing years of steam. Top: Jubilee 4-6-0 No 45673 Keppel makes heavy weather of the last mile to Blea Moor summit with the 9.15 St Pancras – Edinburgh 'Waverley' in the 1960s, only a few years before closure of the Waverley route; Centre upper: One of Polmadie's Britannia Pacifics, No 70051 Dornoch Firth with high-sided tender heads the 'Thames-Clyde' in the early 1960s; Centre lower: During the 1960s ER A3s entered the scene as here with No 60036 Colombo borrowed from Ardsley shed working the morning Leeds-Glasgow train; Bottom: The diesel era, but improbably represented by York Class 40 No D258 heading a rake of Gresley non-gangwayed outer suburban coaches.

A Class 4 2-6-4T simmers in Skipton station.

57

Trans-Pennine freight in the late 1930s: a Stanier 2-8-0 bustles northward past Marley Junction, Keighley. In the second world war soon to come these engines were the mainstay of a freight traffic so intense that trains were often running only a block apart; they were supplemented by both British and US WD 2-8-0s and also by the Riddles WD 2-10-0s.

Class 4F 0-6-0 No 43913 trundles a typically mixed freight of the early 1950s – anything from containers to oil tanks and a couple of high-sided coal wagons – past Bell Busk box on its way north.

An unusual apparition on the Leeds–Carlisle route – one of Wellingborough's Crosti-boilered Class 9 2-10-0s, No 92024, near Keighley with empty Carflats; the picture must have been taken after 1959, the date at which rebuilding of the ten Crosti engines as orthodox steamers began (it was completed in 1961), since No 92024 has had its pre-heater drum removed and is exhausting through the conventional chimney. Non-standard 2-10-0s with a regular Long Drag assignment at this time were the mechanical stoker-fitted trio, Nos 92165-7, specially allocated to Saltley shed for through working on the nightly pair of Birmingham-Carlisle Class C and D merchandise freights.

Caprotti Class 5 4-6-0 No 44755 of Holbeck shed drifts down from Ais Gill summit to Carlisle with a northbound freight, with Wild Boar Fell looming in the background.

Five of the Stanier Class 5 4-6-0 variants
with double chimney, Caprotti valve gear
and roller bearings introduced in 1948 were
despatched to Holbeck shed and soon
afterwards Eric Treacy caught this one in
northbound action near Horton-in-
Ribblesdale.

Its lined black livery admirably maintained,
No 6108 Seaforth Highlander poses at
Hellifield in the mid-1940s during its halt
with a St Pancras–Glasgow express.

Facing top:
Class A3 Pacific No 4472 Flying Scotsman
on the turntable at Steamtown, Carnforth.

Facing bottom:
Frenchman at Carnforth: the privately
preserved No 231.K.22 in double harness
with Class B1 4-6-0 No 1306 Mayflower,
the latter decked out in LNER apple green
livery. No 231.K.22 was one of a series of
Pacifics built by the PLM Railway between
1909 and 1921 and rejuvenated with Dabeg
water economy reheater, ACFI feed water
heater and double blastpipe and chimney in
the 1930s. After the post-war electrification
of their home ground a number of these
four-cylinder compounds were moved to
the SNCF's Nord Region, where they
outlasted the celebrated Collin 'Super-
Pacifics' of Class 231.C.

Overleaf:
In the days before preserved steam was
restricted to specific routes, the preserved
A4 No 4498 Sir Nigel Gresley is run-in on
the West Coast main line; it is leaving an as
yet unelectrified Carlisle station with a
parcels train.

60

Facing page:
*Class 55 No 55021 Argyll & Sutherland
Highlander halts at York with a Kings
Cross-Newcastle train in late 1970s,
shortly before the advent of Inter-City 125
HSTs and the displacement of the 3,300hp
Deltics from the prime East Coast main
line services. York was the final base of the
class before its retirement at the dawn of
1982.*

*No 6108 Seaforth Highlander, one of the
first five Rebuilt Scots to be allocated to
Leeds Holbeck in late 1943, was
photographed shortly after the war's end,
still in lined black livery and without
smoke deflectors, getting away from
Skipton with the southbound 'Thames–
Clyde Express'.*

*A Johnson Class 2F 0-6-0 from
Manningham shed, No 3078, is
surprisingly paired with Stanier Class 5
4-6-0 No 5392 on a local train near
Keighley in the late 1930s.*

A pair of Jubilees, Nos 45691 Orion *and 45714* Revenge, *accelerate the down 'Waverley' away from Hellifield at the end of the 1950s.*

Shortly before its transfer from Holbeck to the LMR in exchange for a Britannia Pacific in 1959 Rebuilt Scot No 46109 Royal Engineer takes the down Waverley along the high fell sides at Dent.

Midland compound and inside-cylinder 4-4-0s were still a common sight on the Leeds–Carlisle line in the 1930s, though their express passenger duty was limited to piloting: here No 422 is useful power for an engineer's train.

Ivatt Class 2 2-6-2T and a northbound stopping train against a backcloth of Pen-y-Ghent.

Eric Treacy cherished this as his favourite
shot of a Jubilee 4-6-0. In BR's lined green
livery No 45573 Newfoundland *climbs
beneath Wild Boar Fell to Ais Gill summit
with the revived Edinburgh–St Pancras
through train (the 'Thames–Forth Express'
disappeared during the war). The post-war
train did not receive a name, the
'Waverley', until 1957.*

Looking towards Ais Gill as No 6108
Seaforth Highlander *pounds up the long
gradient, regulator wide open and on 30
per cent cut-off. 'What a glorious deep-
throated roar the engine was making', Eric
Treacy wrote later.*

THE 'MERSEYSIDE', THE 5.25 AND THE 'TURBO'

Two trains and one locomotive were repeated and celebrated subjects for Eric Treacy's pre-war camera work on Merseyside, a selection of which follows along with one or two of his finest post-war shots in the same locality. The trains were the 10.10 a.m. 'Merseyside Express' and the 5.25 out of Lime Street, and the engine the unique LMS non-condensing geared turbine Pacific No 6202, popularly known as the 'Turbomotive'.

In the second half of the 1930s the 10.10 a.m. and the 5.25 p.m. were the two stellar weekday trains from Liverpool to Euston. When the first Stanier Princess Royal Pacifics took the stage in the spring of 1935 the 5.25, locally tagged the 'Liverpool Flyer', was normally restricted to 10 or 11 coaches. That was because its Royal Scot power was set the fastest LMS schedule of the period, a timing of only 142 minutes for the 152.7 miles from the Crewe stop to its call at Willesden Junction to decant passengers for the North-West London suburbs (that was excised from the schedule shortly before the war). By the last pre-war summer, however, the loading of the 5.25 had gradually inflated to 14 or 15 coaches.

What the Princess Royals could make of that tough assignment was previewed in three June days of 1935, when the newly modified No 6200 was given three consecutive days of heavy load testing on the 10.30 down, normally a very substantial train, and the 5.25 back, the latter specially extended to 15 vehicles for the trials. The last up run was one of the 1930s classics. With 15 coaches of 475 tons gross *Princess Royal* devoured the 152.7 miles from Crewe to Willesden start to stop in a fraction over 129½ minutes, dropping no lower than 57.7 mph on the 1 in 177 out of Crewe and indulging in frequent bursts in the 80s, up to 86.6mph at Kings Langley. Four years later Cecil J. Allen reckoned that performance to have been slightly bettered by the same Pacific with 15 coaches of 500 tons gross. He calculated that No 6200's Edge Hill crew had then passed Willesden (the train no longer stopped there) in the equivalent of 132 minutes net, allowing for one dead stand at Polesworth because of straying sheep and another of 4¼ minutes for signals before Watford Junction.

The 'Merseyside Express' seldom made up to fewer than 14 or 15 cars. With 15 on its gross load was likely to be around 525 tons, because it most unusually embodied two complete dining-car sets to satisfy the heavy meal demand on its down evening leg at 6.5 p.m. from Euston. One set comprised a kitchen car flanked by two open firsts, the other a kitchen-third 12-wheeler and an open third. Another of the 'Merseyside's' distinctions was one of the five first class 10-seater lounge brakes built in 1928, originally for the 'Royal Scot', which featured individual deep leather armchairs and settees in a fully carpeted and expensively wood-panelled saloon. The train included a through Southport portion, which was attached to the front of the up train at Lime Street, but coming back was detached from the rear at a special Edge Hill stop, then taken on to destination via Walton and Bootle. Mossley Hill was a 'Merseyside' call each way, and from there the up train had to cover the 189.7 miles to Euston in 189 minutes.

The rosters covering the 5.25 and the 'Merseyside' were a priority for Pacifics as the LMS stud of 4-6-2s accumulated with the construction of Nos 6202–12. The crew rosters alternated the 5.25 between Edge Hill and Camden men.

No 6202 was originally programmed as a third orthodox Pacific in the 1933 LMS output along with Nos 6200/1, but first-hand investigation of Swedish research and development persuaded Stanier to change course and shape the third Pacific as a turbine-driven machine. First cost would be higher, but the reward was expected to be improved thermal efficiency, less hammer-blow and less wear and tear than in a conventional steam Pacific's cylinders and valves. The main turbine, normally rated at 2,000hp but with 2,600hp potential at high speed, was permanently coupled to the leading driving axle through reduction gearing; a second small turbine was cut in only for working in reverse. Parts standard with those of the 1935 batch of orthodox Pacifics were used to the greatest extent practicable to cut costs; that included the boiler and driving wheels, of which the latter could easily have been made smaller, since the rate of piston rotation at high rail speed was not a concern, so as to accommodate a bigger boiler or ashpan.

The 'Turbomotive' was outstandingly the most successful British steam venture into the unorthodox. Deputed for most of its pre-war career to the London–Liverpool duty embracing the 8.30 or 10.30 down and the fast 5.25 back, it did not match the annual mileage of the standard Princess Royals, but its average of 54,000 was on a par with the general run of British express passenger engines. None of the 13 major failures to which it succumbed undermined the principles of its design. However, the determination to curb cost and avoid complication, such, for instance, as would have been incurred by adoption of condensing equipment, restricted its economy in coal consumption by comparison with a conventional Stanier Pacific to little more than 5 per cent.

Some drivers revelled in the 'Turbo'. 'What a lovely engine she is,' Camden's Laurie Earl once exclaimed. 'Not so much science about the driving, perhaps, turning the valves off one by one instead of the careful adjustment of regulator and cut-off to suit every change of the road, but for continuous strength and speed there is not another engine in her class to touch her.' Earl was one of the drivers involved in the 1936 and 1937 Euston–Glasgow trials of the 'Turbo' on the 'Royal Scot', on one of which No 6202 lifted 17 bogies of 560 tons gross up the 1 in 77 out of Euston without help. On another of the 'Turbo' trips, with the load marginally trimmed to 530 tons, Earl took no more than 36 minutes to cover the 31½ miles from Carlisle to Shap Summit. The crews' main grouse at No 6202 was that its soft exhaust let smoke drift into their cab, a failing which the LMS strangely left untended until 1939, when smoke deflectors were at last fitted to the 'Turbo'.

At the outbreak of war the 'Turbo' was stored, but it resumed work briefly in 1941, only to suffer a failure that side-tracked it until 1942. Thereafter its employment was decidedly spasmodic. Finally, in 1952, when the engine had 440,000 miles under its belt, the Railway Executive's mechanical engineering chief, Robin Riddles, ruled that the cost of keeping No 6202 mobile, and by then it needed a new main turbine, could not be justified. It was rebuilt as an orthodox steam locomotive, with four Duchess-type cylinders to be fed by a Princess Royal boiler, and named *Princess Anne*. As such it was the most powerful of the LMS Pacifics in tractive effort terms. Alas, scarcely had it been run in before it was damaged beyond repair in the appalling Harrow & Wealdstone double collision of 8 October 1952.

Overleaf:
Ex-LNW Precursor 4-4-0 No 25188 Marquis, a Chester engine, leans to the curve at Edge Hill as it heads for North Wales with a parcels train. When this photograph was taken in the mid-1930s only 30 of the 130-strong class were still active; just one of them, No 25297 Sirocco, survived to become a BR machine, but it was scrapped in 1948.

The lined black livery which Robin Riddles wanted to apply to all express passenger locomotives when BR was formed is displayed by Stanier Pacific No 6254 City of Stoke-on-Trent, posing at Edge Hill sheds soon after the war.

In the late 1930s some rebuilt Claughton 4-6-0s were still shedded at Edge Hill. This is No 5946 Duke of Connaught, *making a fuss of the climb away from Edge Hill with a summer holiday extra.*

Chester-based No 25310 Thunderer, *an ex-LNW Precursor 4-4-0, heads for home past Wavertree with a Liverpool–Holyhead train of the mid-1930s.*

One of the LNWR's 1911-built 0-8-2 shunting tanks, No 7877, leaves the Edge Hill yard, or 'Gridiron', with a Garston freight in the late 1930s, when this yard was generating 50–60 trains a day, to destinations ranging from Carlisle and Kendal to Burton and Abergavenny.

One of the Kitson-built LMS Class 0F 0-4-0STs of 1932, No 7002, shedded at Edge Hill, poses at its home alongside Farnley Junction Jubilee 4-6-0 No 5704 Leviathan.

Patricroft Jubilee 4-6-0 No 5599
Bechuanaland *bustles past Edge Hill with
one of the limited-stop expresses of the
1930s from Lime Street to Manchester
Exchange; this may well have been the 12
noon, allowed 39 minutes for the 31½-mile
run inclusive of a stop at St Helens
Junction, as opposed to today's diesel age
standard of 43 minutes from Lime Street to
Manchester Victoria.*

Crewe-based Jubilee 4-6-0 No 5603
Solomon Islands *rouses the cutting echoes
as it lifts a London train out of Lime Street
in the late 1930s.*

Princess Royal Pacific No 6201 Princess Elizabeth battles past Edge Hill with the heavy 'Merseyside Express'; immediately behind the tender are the two through coaches from Southport, while the fifth vehicle is the kitchen-third 12-wheeler. This photograph is probably dated 1936, when No 6201 had just acquired a high-. sided tender of the pattern fitted new to Nos 6202–12, but before its rebuilding with a high-superheat boiler that year.

The 'Turbomotive' rebuilt in 1952 as orthodox four-cylinder 4-6-2 No 46202 Princess Anne. The train it powers past Wavertree, the up 'Red Rose', was the post-war 5.25 to Euston, which was one of those newly named and assigned the first sets of BR standard Mk I coaches in Festival of Britain year, 1951 (the down 'Red Rose' was the 12.5 p.m. from Euston). But in 1952 the 5.25 was allowed as much as 17 minutes more for its Crewe–Euston run than the pre-war counterpart.

The rebuilt 'Turbomotive', No 46202 Princess Anne, is prepared for the London run at Edge Hill.

No 6202, the 'Turbomotive', as built,
heads the 5.25 to Euston past Wavertree.
The casing above the leading bogie on this
side of the engine housed the small reverse
turbine, that on the hidden nearside of the
4-6-2 its main forward turbine.

80

Facing:
*The 15-inch gauge Ravenglass & Eskdale
Railway was originally put down as a 3ft-
gauge quarry line in 1873, acquired in 1915
and converted to its present gauge by an
associate company of the model builders,
Bassett-Lowke, and since 1953 operated by
a preservation organisation. The 2-8-2
River Mite is one of its newest
locomotives, ordered from a York builder
in 1966.*

Overleaf:
*The North Yorkshire Moors Railway runs
from a junction with BR's Whitby–
Middlesbrough line at Grosmont to
Pickering, traversing magnificent moorland
scenery. These two 0-6-2Ts came from the
National Coal Board, whose Nos 5 and 29
they were, and originally worked at
Lambton Colliery; they are taking a
breather at Grosmont.*

One of the most bizarre features of the Railway Executive's locomotive building programme in the early years of BR was its endorsement of the construction in 1951 of 28 more shunting engines to an NER design of 1898 by Wilson Worsdell; this type, which became the LNER Class J72 0-6-0T, was in fact the only British type known to have been built to the same design in different batches over as long a period as half a century. Though it has been given North Eastern Railway livery this engine, named Joem by its preservation owners and here seen on the Derwent Valley Light Railway, was actually one of the 1951 BR-built batch and was formerly BR No 69023.

A streamliner takes the 5.25 to Euston past Wavertree, blue-and-silver liveried No 6220 Coronation herself. This engine became No 6229 in 1939, when the real No 6229 was chosen for the 'Coronation Scot's' US trip and assumed No 6220's number and name.

Why is a Camden Pacific, No 6208 Princess
Helena Victoria, on a Liverpool-West of
England express, liberally infused with
GWR coaching stock? To judge from its
cleanliness one would wager that the
Princess in this Edge Hill scene was
running in after attention at Crewe.

WESTERN INTERLUDE

The Western Region, or, indeed, the Great Western before, it was not really Eric Treacy's territory hence the rather sparse coverage of GWR subjects. Nevertheless Treacy's camera certainly captured Great Western locomotives, particularly where they ran in areas more familiar to him. Moreover he also had a fairly free run around Paddington, particularly the servicing depot at Ranelagh Bridge which was by Royal Oak station. One tends to look in vain, though, for Treacy negatives down typical Great Western branches and the bulk of his shots are of express passenger power, particularly the Kings, Castles, even the earlier Stars.

In this section we have a variety of Great Western types leaving Paddington, even a diesel age shot of the now historic Blue Pullmans, paired with a shot of a Western Class diesel as far west as Bristol, well beyond Treacy's normal outings.

But the unusual has not been forgotten and we see a Great Western King on Eastern Region territory during the 1948 locomotive exchanges and yet again *Clun Castle* at Leeds during a series of special trains at work in 1967, very much part of the preservation era.

The dramatic shot of a Great Western County 4-6-0 included in this section was one of several Eric Treacy took of this class, not surprisingly, because a substantial part of his immediate post-war GW photography was in the Chester and Shrewsbury area; and in the first few years after the debut of the 30 County engines in 1945-7 they worked principally on the Paddington-Wolverhampton -Birkenhead and Plymouth-Penzance routes.

Castle class 4-6-0 No 5070 Sir Daniel
Gooch *leaving Paddington with a fast train
for Reading, Oxford and Worcester – the
route of the Cathedrals Express.*

Castle 4-6-0 No 5075 Wellington *at Chester
in the 1950s.*

Facing page, top:
*An up express near Chester, as usual in the
later 1950s and early 1960s Castle hauled,
here by No 5092* Tresco Abbey. *Note the
second vehicle is a GWR six-wheel bogie
dining car and, a sign of the times, the
third is an ex LMS coach.*

Facing page, bottom:
*One of the last express engines to be built
by the Great Western Railway. A very dirty
No 7017* G.J. Churchward, *complete with
straight sided Hawksworth tender, makes
its way south on a September evening.*

88

Facing page, top:
The Western Region provided King class
No 6018 King Henry VI *as its
representative to run trials on the Eastern
Region from Kings Cross to Leeds and
back in 1948. True to tradition everything
remained Great Western from the white-
painted spare headlamps on the running
plate to the old company's initials on the
tender. It was photographed on the climb
from Beeston to Ardsley.*

Facing page, bottom:
One of the Paddington to Birkenhead via
Birmingham and Wolverhampton trains
awaits the green at the London terminus.
Timings on these trains were not as fast as
those on the LMS route as many stopped at
Banbury in both directions. The
locomotive is No 6006 King George I.

*Shrewsbury-based Star 4-6-0 No 4061
Glastonbury Abbey pulls out of Chester
with a Paddington–Birkenhead express in
the early 1950s.*

*Chester station with Churchward's Star
class 4-6-0 No 4040 Queen Boadicea on the
northern leg of one of the Birkenhead–
Paddington trains via Birmingham. Engines
were changed at Wolverhampton (Low
Level) when a King class 4-6-0 took over
for the journey to London.*

Presumably deputising for a failed King or Castle, a green-liveried Reading Hall, No 6923 Croxteth Hall, gets a Paddington–Birmingham–Birkenhead express on the move from Shrewsbury in the 1950s.

One of Cardiff Canton's stud, No 5007 Rougemont Castle, makes a smart exit from Paddington with a South Wales express in the 1950s. The double slips which studded the track layout of the Paddington approaches in the steam era have been replaced by ladder pointwork in the terminal's subsequent resignalling.

Facing page:
Soon after the second world war a grimy GWR Country 4-6-0, No 1016 County of Hants, bursts from one of the Chester tunnels with a Birkenhead–Paddington express. At the time No 1016 was one of a quintet of Counties based at Wolverhampton's Stafford Road shed.

The record breaking No 7029 Clun Castle on foreign territory, at Holbeck near Leeds during one of its journeys over the Eastern Region in 1967. The train was diesel hauled from London (Kings Cross) to Peterborough where the Castle took over for the run to Carlisle via Settle. It was based at Peterborough shed during its sojourn on the Eastern under the care of the then ER Divisional Manager, London, Richard Hardy.

Western enginemen never made much of the BR Britannia Pacifics until Nos 70025-9 were assigned to Cardiff Canton shed in the autumn of 1952. The results were encouraging enough by the start of 1957 for the shed to be cleared of Castles and made instead the sole base of WR Britannias. Round about then Eric Treacy pictured No 70026 Polar Star leaving Paddington with the 1.55 p.m. to Pembroke Dock.

Western Wanderer: one of the special excursions organised to mark the coming end of WR diesel-hydraulic locomotives. No D1067 Western Druid is shown here at Bristol Temple Meads, a spot normally well out of Treacy territory.

Paddington at the close of the 1960s. Standing at Platform 6 is the down evening 'Bristol Pullman', formed of the two former 'Midland Pullman' six-car diesel units working in multiple. They were transferred to the WR in the spring of 1967 and for the first two years were split to furnish separate midday Bristol and Oxford return Pullman services from Paddington between their up morning and down evening twin-unit operations between Bristol and Paddington. All 'Blue Pullman' services were abandoned in the spring of 1973.

97

Another Chester scene in the immediate
post-war period: framed by characteristic
LNWR semaphores, WR 2-6-0 No 7319 of
Shrewsbury shed restarts a Birkenhead–
Paddington train.

Ranelagh Bridge with a King waiting for its next working back to Wolverhampton.

Tyseley shed Birmingham. Side by side are two preserved 4-6-0s representing express power used between that city and London during the later years. On the left is LMS Stanier Jubilee class 4-6-0 No 5593 Kolhapur and on the right GWR No 7029 Clun Castle.

Overleaf:
King 4-6-0 No 6011 King James I leaves Paddington with a South Wales express. The train is a mixture of styles with the coaches, while painted blood and custard, carrying GWR type destination boards.

CENTRAL TO WESTGATE

Aesthetically, the old Leeds Central station was no beauty. That was scarcely surprising considering its chequered history. The four companies which converged on Leeds from Manchester via Dewsbury, from the Calder Valley, from Thirsk and from Wakefield in the mid-1840s had originally conceived a monumental structure that would concentrate all their traffic. But they fell out over detail. They did so yet again over a less ambitious but still impressive scheme – the structure would have been 900ft long and 400ft wide – which was drafted by John Hawkshaw in 1848.

At last an economy plan was agreed in 1849 and building began, but more dissension and Byzantine manœuvring for routes into the city, plus a serious accident in the half-completed station that was held to require extensive revision of the scheme, deferred completion until 1857. In the subsequent 110 years of its life the cramped station saw little improvement, save that some extra platform length was squeezed out of the station's throat layout, some bay platforms were added and the roof raised.

But the exit from Leeds Central was heaven-sent to a photographer as gifted in portraying the steam locomotive *in extremis* as Eric Treacy. Right from the platform end a departing Pacific struck 1 in 100 up. The slope eased briefly to 1 in 400 through Holbeck High Level, but then stiffened to a fierce 1 in 50 to the bend past Copley Hill shed. Though A4s starred in many of Eric's most spectacular Leeds Central shots, they were almost all Kings Cross-based Pacifics. Copley Hill never had an A4 on its own allocation. At the time Eric was practising in the West Riding A1s were Copley Hill's front-rank power, backed up by A3s as yet to be transformed with double chimneys and blastpipes. Unlike Kings Cross, Copley Hill never assigned its Pacifics to specific rosters or to nominated crews.

Beyond Copley Hill a Pacific had only a mile of down-grade to recover wind before confronting $3\frac{1}{4}$ miles of 1 in 100 up to Ardsley, the freight engine shed at which two or three A1s and A3s had to pass some inglorious months on parcels and goods duty near the end of their days when Deltics had supplanted them on the East Coast main line. Ardsley at last brought relief for the hard-pressed Pacific starting cold from Leeds as the line turned down at 1 in 122 to Lofthouse, steepening to 1 in 100 for the final approach to Wakefield's noble Westgate station, with its elegant Italianate frontage and 97ft-high clock tower. Even a non-stop working through Wakefield had no scope for speed on the slope, though, because in the steam age the Wakefield–Leeds Central stretch was severely speed-restricted. A 25mph limit was in force over the famous 99-arch Calder Valley viaduct on the Doncaster side of Westgate and through the station, followed by a 50mph limit to Lofthouse North Junction and no more than 60mph thence to Wortley South Junction and a drastically slow entrance to the city of Leeds.

The original non-Pullman 'White Rose' in the early 1950s, pausing at Wakefield Westgate on its up journey with Doncaster-based Class A3 No 60046 Diamond Jubilee in charge.

Grantham-based Class A4 No 60026 Miles Beevor gets a grip of the up 'Yorkshire Pullman' at Leeds Central in 1951.

No 60123 H. A. Ivatt *was one of two Class A1 Pacifics based at Ardsley in 1951, principally for overnight parcels and fast freight turns from the West Riding to London, the return workings of which were the 1.18 and 7.15 p.m. passenger expresses from Kings Cross. It was probably a semi-fast which No 60123 was heading out of Leeds Central in this picture.*

The 4.50 p.m. Leeds–Doncaster was one of the last regular steam workings out of Leeds Central station; a Deltic diesel's roof looms behind the train as it is taken out of Central station by Class A1 4-6-2 No 60130 Kestrel.

Another Class A1, No 60139 Sea Eagle, pulls out of Leeds Central with a Doncaster train in the 1950s.

Facing page: Running-in after overhaul an immaculate York A1, No 60146 Peregrine, prepares for an easygoing return to Doncaster with a semi-fast from Leeds Central.

Facing page:
Another 1951 shot at Copley Hill as the local A1 No 60141 Abbotsford *heads for London with the up 'Queen of Scots'.*

A couple of WD 2-8-0s potter about Ardsley shed yard as Class 55 No D9000 Royal Scots Grey *passes with the dawn 'Queen of Scots', probably in the 1961 summer, the train's first with new Metro-Cammell Pullmans. The train had only three more years to run; an anachronism as an Anglo-Scottish train after the 1963 launch of the intensive Deltic regular-interval Kings Cross-Newcastle-Edinburgh timetable, it was transmuted into the Kings Cross-Leeds-Harrogate/Bradford 'White Rose' Pullman in 1964.*

Class A1 No 60126 Sir Vincent Raven, *a Heaton engine all its life until its final three years and a few months, spent at York, winds the northbound 'Queen of Scots' out of Leeds Central in 1951, making for the curve down to Holbeck Geldard Junction and the Midland main line to the north, which it will soon leave to head for Harrogate.*

Another 1951 departure from Leeds
Central: Class A1 4-6-2 No 60114 W. P.
Allen, *then a Copley Hill Pacific and still
with its original unlipped chimney, starts
the mid-afternoon 'White Rose' for Kings
Cross. The leading Gresley coach is still in
LNER varnished teak livery.*

Leeds Central in 1948, with Class A3 4-6-2
No 56 Centenary, *restored from wartime
black to LNER green the previous year,
pulling out on a London train.*

Class A4 No 60010 Dominion of Canada
*heads a Kings Cross express past Wortley
in the early 1950s, when much of its train
was still in LNER livery. The bell,
presented by the Canadian Pacific Railway,
was retained until the A4 was rebuilt with
a double chimney in the late 1950s; at first
it was operable by steam power, but that
was disconnected before the war after a
driver working the engine on the down
'Coronation' had rung the bell leaving
Kings Cross, then been unable to stop it
until he reached York and found a way of
cutting off the steam supply.*

Leeds Central line-up in the early 1950s –
Class N1 0-6-2T No 69483, Class J50 0-6-0T
No 68978 and Class A3 4-6-2 No 60055
Woolwinder. The West Riding was the last
stronghold of the N1s, which covered local
workings on the ex-GN lines right up to
the dmus' advent in 1955; at the start of
1956 all but three of the survivors were in
the area, seven of them at Bradford, three
at Copley Hill and eight at Ardsley.

During the 1950s Ardsley had one or two
ex-Great Central Class C13 4-4-2Ts for
short-haul passenger duty and one of the
type, the push-pull fitted No 67433,
appears on a Leeds Central local, restarting
from Holbeck High Level.

Facing page:
Copley Hill Class B1 4-6-0 No 61387
attacks the 1 in 50 from Holbeck up to
Copley Hill with a Leeds–Cleethorpes train
in 1951.

LINES FROM LEEDS CITY

You would not normally come across a Gresley A4 or a Stanier Pacific in Leeds City station in the 1950s, but it was a meeting-place of every other principal Eastern and London Midland express passenger type, and a great deal more besides. You needed a photographer's track permit, though, to make as much of the varied power on view as Eric Treacy did.

City did not become an integrated station until 1938. The oldest half was the Wellington station, solidified from a temporary into a permanent structure in 1850, which in the ensuing decade attempted to cope with practically every train service into and out of the city bar the Great Northern's. The North Eastern and London & North Western soon had enough of the mounting congestion and early in the 1860s the NER planned its elevated entry from Marsh Lane to a new station, on the south side of Wellington, which would be erected in partnership with the LNWR.

The result, known as Leeds New, which was constructed on a honeycomb of vaults above the River Aire and a branch of the Leeds & Liverpool Canal, took over all NER and LNWR traffic in 1869. That left the Midland in occupation of Wellington next door and Leeds Central to the GNR and LNWR, though for years afterward the LNWR religiously ran one train a year into and out of Central to underscore its retention of part-ownership of that station. The GNR exchanged passengers with the MR and NER at the superimposed Holbeck High and Low Level stations.

The next major project was the LNWR's construction of its New Line exit from the western end of New station to Wortley. This was to get its trains clear of the over-intensively used stretch of the Midland between Leeds and Whitehall junctions, which was also the path of NER trains to and from Harrogate. It was inaugurated in 1882. Three years later Leeds' fourth locomotive shed, Farnley Junction, sprang up alongside the line, joining the Midland's Holbeck, the NER's Neville Hill and the GNR's Copley Hill.

After 1923 Leeds New station remained in joint ownership, now by the LMS and LNER, but neither moved to integrate its offices with those of Wellington, let alone satisfy the perennial pressure for absorption of all Leeds passenger business in one station, until the eve of the last war. Then at last, in the spring of 1938, Wellington and New were integrated by a new concourse with attendant facilities that included bathrooms and dressing rooms as well as the more expected offices, and as part of a scheme that also embodied construction of the railway-owned Queens Hotel. At the same time Wellington and New were renamed Leeds City North and South respectively. Considered as one station, Leeds City now became one of the country's most extensive, covering 19½ acres and disposing of 16 platforms.

The LMS and LNER took a fresh look at the case for concentrating Leeds' passenger traffic on one station in the last war's closing months but recoiled at the cost. Flush with Modernisation Plan capital, however, the BTC launched just such a plan in 1959. Costed at £4½ millions, it was programmed for completion in 1963–4, but after various traumas it was not finished, and then in emasculated form, until 1967.

The reconstruction was stopped dead from July 1961 to March 1963 by the freeze of several major, high-cost projects, including the LMR ac electrification, which Conservative Transport Minister Ernest Marples ordered after the critical reappraisals of BR's investment decisions at the end of the 1950s and as a prelude to Beeching's appointment to a newly-constituted BRB. One of Beeching's early moves was an abortive attempt to persuade Leeds' civic authorities to underwrite some of the cost of the new Leeds City station.

In the reorganisation some of the main line exits photographed by Eric Treacy in the 1950s disappeared. After an early scheme to connect the ex-GN approach from Doncaster to the ex-LNW Leeds–Huddersfield line between Morley Low and Farnley Junction had been discarded, the BR planners built the 1 in 50 Geldard curve from Copley Hill down to the onetime LNWR New Line approach on viaduct to Leeds City East Junction. The displaced Huddersfield–Manchester trains were given a new route to Farnley Junction from Whitehall Junction via the former LNWR Copley Hill carriage yard, and the Wellington area of Leeds City station was transmuted into a parcels depot.

A double-headed train from the North-West to the North-East awaits the flag at Leeds City, in this case with York Class B1 4-6-0 No 61016 Impala *fronting a Class V2 2-6-2.*

Rebuilt Scot No 46112 Sherwood Forester
storms past Wortley North box on its way
out of Leeds with a Glasgow express via
Ais Gill in the early 1950s.

Overleaf:
On the Keighley & Worth Valley Railway,
Britain's second oldest former BR
preserved passenger line, the five-mile
branch from Keighley to Oxenhope; since
the start of its new era in 1968 it has
become known countrywide as the setting
for countless video productions, from films
such as The Railway Children and Yanks
to TV commercials. Here an afternoon
train from Keighley approaches Oxenhope
behind Ivatt Class 2 2-6-2T No 41241,
which the K&WVR has styled in LMS
crimson lake.

Facing top:
Bustle at the Keighley & Worth Valley's
Haworth headquarters: locomotives on
view include ex-GWR 0-6-0PT No 5775 in
the livery of London Transport, with
which it ended its public career as No L89;
'Black Five' 4-6-0 No 45212; BR Class 9
2-10-0 No 92220 Evening Star; and ex-
L&YR 0-4-0ST No 51218.

Facing bottom:
No 70032, seen towards the end of its
career, shorn of its Tennyson nameplates,
was one of the 1953 batch of Britannia
Pacifics. It was one of the LMR's stud of
the engines, originally allocated to
Holyhead, where its small BR1-type tender
was quickly found inadequate for the
London run with the 'Irish Mail', and then
reassigned to Manchester's Longsight shed,
where it passed most its career.

GOODS TRAINS TO STOP
TO PIN DOWN BRAKES

A filthy 'Black Five' 4-6-0, No 45372, trundles northwards from Carlisle past Kingmoor shed with mixed freight. The train is traversing the goods line connections from the Waverley route Carlisle exit, which were a component of the huge layout reorganisation complementary to the construction of the automated marshalling yard north of Carlisle. That was ordered pre-Beeching under the LMR's 1959 Freight Plan, which envisaged full-scale perpetuation of wagonload freight working and was concerned to eliminate the costly trip working between Carlisle's former nine yards. Completed in 1962 at a cost of £4½ millions in contemporary money, Carlisle yard was a white elephant within a decade.

In the second half of the 1950s one of Carlisle Upperby's Jubilee 4-6-0s, No 45696 Arethusa, eases an express over the Midland route from Glasgow past Holbeck Low Level. In the background a 'Jinty' 0-6-0T lifts a rake of merchandise wagons from Wellington Street goods depot.

121

Facing page:
A3 driver's view of the Midland exit to the north, as double-chimney No 60081 Shotover, *a Neville Hill Pacific for almost all its post-war life, so evidently only on loan to Holbeck when Eric Treacy rode her in 1961, passes Holbeck Low Level.*

In the first half of the 1950s the B16 class 4-6-0s were almost equally shared between York and Neville Hill sheds, with the exception of a solitary outcast at Scarborough. No 61413 of Neville Hill, framed at Leeds City, was one of the unrebuilt Class B16/1s.

An early post-nationalisation scene at Leeds City Junction, as Rebuilt Scot 4-6-0 No 46133 The Green Howards *emerges from Wellington station and forks right for Carlisle, away from the Midland route to the south, en route to Glasgow.*

Facing page, top:
Longsight Jubilee No 45595 Southern Rhodesia *and Edge Hill Royal Scot No 46124* London Scottish *head for home in the early 1950s, pulling out of Leeds City with a Newcastle–Liverpool express.*

Facing page, bottom:
It is the early 1960s and the West Riding's Class D49 4-4-0s have been superseded by BR standard Class 4 2-6-4Ts, of which Neville Hill's No 80118 is mobilised to assist double-chimney Class A3 4-6-2 No 60082 Neil Gow *to Harrogate with a Liverpool–Newcastle train.*

A Newcastle–Liverpool express of the early 1950s, with LNER and BR stock sharing crimson-and-cream livery, passes Leeds City West box behind Longsight Patriot 4-6-0 No 45519 Lady Godiva and a Royal Scot 4-6-0.

In the mid-1950s Neville Hill shed's Class A3 Pacific No 60074 Harvester, with Class D49/2 4-4-0 No 62749 The Cottesmore start a Liverpool–Newcastle train out of Leeds City. The 4-4-0, one of Starbeck's allocation, will assist the Pacific as far as Harrogate, to help the latter up the taxing five-mile bank to Moseley Siding, beyond Horsforth, almost all of it graded at 1 in 100.

125

Soon after nationalisation a Manningham-based compound 4-4-0, No 41080, bustles out of the Midland side of Leeds City with a Bradford train.

Class 4 2-6-4T No 42052 on Holbeck shed turntable.

126

Soon after nationalisation a Neville Hill
Class G5 0-4-4T, No 67262, snakes out of
Leeds City with a Harrogate local.

In the 1930s the North Eastern Area of the
LNER was the most progressive rail sector
in the country in the development of
thumb-switch interlocking panels, as
distinct from power interlocking lever
frames. Leeds West box had the switches
for both points and signals (each switch
operated an individual apparatus – there
was no route-setting) mounted on its
layout diagram, but at Leeds East the
points were operated mechanically.

It is 1960 and Class A3 Pacifics have been
drafted to Holbeck shed for Settle-Carlisle
duty. One of the less euphoniously named
Class A3s, No 60088 Book Law (the 1927
St Leger winner), now a double-chimney
engine, thrusts away from Holbeck with
the northbound 'Thames–Clyde Express'.

CAUGHT ON THE CURVE – YORK AND NEWCASTLE

Some of the steam age's most awesome pyrotechnics were staged at York and Newcastle. The tight curve of York's No 9 platform and the S-bend of Newcastle Central's principal down platform were two of the most vicious places in the country at which to restart a heavy northbound train. So often they were the acid test of enginemanship that distinguished the footplate craftsman from the ham-handed time-server; the late W.A. Tuplin once penned a vivid comparison of the two extremes of driving method as witnessed at York's No 9 platform.

First Tuplin pictured an A3 driver overshooting the water hydrant and having to set back slightly to align his tender water-hole with the pipe. Snapping on his brake at the critical moment while he is in reverse, this driving inevitably lets the momentum of the train behind tighten every coupling in it. So, when he gets the flag and wrenches his regulator far too widely open, the 15-coach train expectedly holds firm on the curve and the A3's wheels all too easily fly on rails superbly polished by hosts of similarly mishandled engines. A volcanic spew of dirty smoke and cinders mushrooms against the great arched roof and the station trembles to a horrifying, frustrated roar of three-cylinder exhaust.

Pushing and tugging at a refractory regulator, the driver at last manages to quieten his Pacific. But he fails to get the regulator open again just before the slip is halted, which he should do so as to get steam into the cylinders and encourage the forward surge of the wheels once they have re-established a grip. The moment the slip has been controlled, the Pacific duly makes fractional ground: but all that does, with no steam at the pistons, is to tighten the couplings yet again.

The driver tries again. This time the Pacific just wheezes. The driver has been caught in the trap that a three-cylinder engine with cut-off limited to 65 per cent is always prone to spring, because it has six almost dead positions in each driving wheel revolution. As Tuplin explained it, 'when one piston has almost reached the end of its stroke, pressure on it by steam admitted by the lead of the valve opposes rotation. Another piston has passed the 65 per cent point and no steam gets to it, whilst the third piston has full steam pressure behind it, but its crank presents only about 75 per cent of its maximum leverage. The result is that the starting effort is about a quarter of the normal amount. This is not enough to start a heavy train on a long curve, so the Pacific refuses.'

Nothing for it but to reverse. More cacophony as the eager boiler, denied work, lifts its safety valves and the fireman opens the cylinder cocks to void steam admitted for forward running. The driver tugs the regulator and the A3 heaves its train back about a foot, then slips in that direction too. More work on the reverser, another wrench on the regulator, and the wretched A3 at last gets a hold of its train, but with the foot of the reversal regained its faltering advance all but stops at the same dead point in its three-cylinder cycle.

Thank heaven, this time just enough steam pressure has been built up in the cylinders to edge the Pacific through it. Then, when the wheels have revolved to the high point of the cycle, away they go in another high-speed, treble fortissimo slip. With two or three more slips the labouring A3 eventually makes it past the adjoining Scarborough line diamonds. And some five minutes after its crew were given the right-away the last of its 14 coaches recedes from view behind the engine shed yard.

How should it have been done? According to Tuplin, the skilled driver aiming to take water from that York Platform 9 stand-pipe put his Pacific into reverse as he approached it. That way he would brake the train to a precisely judged stand with all its coaches pressed up against the tender, buffer springs compressed and all outer wheel flanges pressed against the curve's outer rail. Then the driver would apply his tender brake so that the train would be held tight, ready for the start, even when he released its vacuum brakes.

At the right-away the Pacific would still be in reverse. So at the first gentle opening of the regulator, with the fireman unwinding the tender brake, the engine would compress the nearest buffer springs to the maximum. Then it was into forward gear, a brief venting of the cylinder cocks to expel back-pressing steam, and regulator open again. With the impetus of expanding buffer springs and without the drag of binding wheel flanges, the Pacific would get its train decisively on the move.

Now the fireman would lend his driver a hand on the regulator. Whenever the Pacific's pace slowed at the dead point in each cycle of the stroke the two men, working as one with the instinct born of dedicated teamwork, would open the regulator wider, then pull it back as soon as the engine resumed its forward surge. With the strength of four arms it was much easier to make rapid and finely graded adjustments of a Gresley engine's often stiff regulator handle, thereby keeping steam pressure just below the level at which the slow-moving Pacific would be driven into a slip. And so, with barely an anxious second, and without hazarding any eardrums on No 9 platform, this Pacific would forge sure-footed to the Scarborough crossing and away to Newcastle.

Heaton Class A3 No 60073 St Gatien,
heading a Liverpool–Newcastle express
from Leeds, refills its tank at York's No 9
platform standpipe.

Another of York's Class V2 2-6-2s, No
60839, restarts a Liverpool–Newcastle train
from its home city in the early 1950s.

In the opening years of nationalisation
Heaton Class A3 No 60077 The White
Knight heads a northbound express away
from York.

Class A3 Pacific No 60082 Neil Gow, *a North Eastern-based engine throughout its career, heads a Kings Cross express out of York in the 1950s; waiting for the road with southbound freight, on the left are a Class O4/8 2-8-0 and a Class B16/3 4-6-0*

A Class J25 0-6-0 of York shed trundles a lightweight engineers' train under Holgate bridge south of York station, passing Class O2 2-8-0 No 63953.

The North Eastern Railway survives intact, coaches as well as locomotive, in the early years of nationalisation: Selby's Class D20 4-4-0 No 62343 returns home on a stopping train from York.

A Sheffield train of the early 1950s departs from York behind Class D11/1 4-4-0 No 62663 Prince Albert, *then shedded at Darnall.*

Overleaf:
Probably a 1949 or 1950 view of York's north end as the local shed's Class V2 2-6-2 No 60979 removes empty stock from the station past one of the Scottish Region's Class A2 Pacifics, No 60531 Bahram, *since the sempahore signals indicate that the York resignalling is not complete; that was achieved in 1951.*

A shot of Class D49/2 No 62751 The
Albrighton, *a Scarborough engine at the
end of the 1940s, after arrival at York with
a train from its home town. A Class V2
2-6-2 stands on the through road.*

A pair of Class D49 4-4-0s with No 62751
The Albrighton *leading heads a
Scarborough–Leeds train out of York.*

York Class V2 2-6-2 No 60978 *clatters over the famous diamonds at the north end of Newcastle Central (the crossings are scheduled for elimination in a resignalling and layout reorganisation BR hopes to execute in the 1980s) with southbound freight empties.*

Class A2/2 Pacific No 60505 Thane of Fife, *one of Thompson's ill-judged rebuilds of Gresley's Class P2 2-8-2s, winds a Newcastle–Kings Cross express past Gateshead in the early 1950s. It was a New England engine from 1949 to withdrawal.*

Overleaf:
Heaton Class A3 Pacific No 60092 Fairway *eases a Kings Cross express out of Newcastle in the early 1950s, framed by what used to be one of the most bewildering signal gantries in the country, and still was in early BR days, despite the abandonment of some of its posts and the replacement of most of its NER lower-quadrants by upper-quadrants.*

Haymarket Class A3 No 60037 Hyperion takes over an express from London at Newcastle for the last lap to Edinburgh.

Haymarket Class A4 Pacific No 60012 Commonwealth of Australia backs on to a northbound express at Newcastle in the 1950s.

THE SOUTHERN AT HOME AND AWAY

With the major exception of some early post-war work in the neighbourhood of Tonbridge, Eric Treacy's Southern photography focussed almost exclusively on the Region's London termini and their approaches. Some of the most spectacular ascents of Grosvenor bank ever frozen on film derive from the happy coincidence of Victoria station's proximity to the chambers of Westminster where the Church of England hierarchy assembled in periodical conclave. Eric was adept at exploiting any legitimate break in the proceedings for a sprint to the lineside and back. Many a tedious conference, he once wrote, vouchsafed a few off-duty moments that in turn yielded their quota of worthwhile pictures; thus 'I learned never to travel without permits and camera – for you never knew!'

That way, too, Waterloo was the principal setting other than his home territory of the West Riding for most of his records of the 1948 Locomotive Exchanges, a selection of which follow. Eric had aimed to cover a great deal more of these fascinating locomotive switches. Possessed of the whole season's running order, he had worked out an itinerary covering most of it from ideal locations, only to find when he compared the plan with his diary that official engagements clashed with most of it. Moreover, petrol for pleasure driving was still rationed and Eric was not the man to use his professional allocation to reach a camera vantage point unless he had an official engagement close by. To crown all, his bicycle had just been stolen from outside his house.

Eric's shots of the strangers at Waterloo feature the unquestioned star of the trials on the Waterloo–Exeter main line, Rebuilt Scot 4-6-0 No 46154 *The Hussar*. Eric pictured the LM 4-6-0 on one of its preliminary trips with the down 'Atlantic Coast Express'. Later, during the test proper with dynamometer car on 18 June 1948 and heading a packed up train of 515 tons gross, the Scot outperformed all its Pacific rivals on the $11\frac{1}{4}$-mile climb from the Axminster start to the Hewish summit, parts of which are as steep as 1 in 120. Reaching almost 60mph on the brief level at Chard Junction, the Scot's Driver Brooker carried the final 6.2 miles to the crest at an average of 55.1mph. On the 1 in 200 stretch of the climb the dynamometer car recorded a stunning drawbar horsepower of 1,782, equivalent to 21hp/ton power/engine weight ratio. No less creditable was the fact that it was all done with a cut-off no more than 30 per cent, the regulator about one-quarter open and working pressure held between 225 and 242 lb/sq in.

143

A Treacy classic: most likely photographed in the summer of 1947, still unnamed and before modification of smoke deflectors and cab to improve the driver's forward visibility, Bulleid West Country Pacific No 21C139 of Stewarts Lane shed attacks the 1 in 62 Grosvenor bank out of Victoria with a Kent Coast train.

Another 1947 summer scene on Grosvenor bank: Class L 4-4-0 No 1773 makes a manful climb with a Kent Coast extra.

The Pullmans which the SR had featured in some Kent Coast trains were at first not restored after the war, but in May 1948 the all-Pullman 'Thanet Belle' was inaugurated as a summer service between Victoria and Ramsgate, and Pullmans were included in its winter counterpart of otherwise standard SR stock. In the train's first year Battle of Britain Pacific No 21C154 Lord Beaverbrook moves it out of Victoria. To mark the addition of a Canterbury portion (which was a commercial failure and lasted only one season) in 1951, the train was renamed the 'Kentish Belle'.

Overleaf:
The 'Golden Arrow' leaves Victoria just before the second world war, when the train had had to surrender its all-Pullman exclusivity because its premium-fare traffic had declined after the slump earlier in the decade. Heading the train is Lord Nelson 4-6-0 No 863 Lord Rodney, the first of the class to be fitted with Lemaître blastpipe and large diameter chimney (in the summer of 1938). No 863 was also one of the first four Nelsons to be repainted in Bulleid's olive green livery (later superseded by malachite green), all on Continental duty in 1939.

On one of its preliminary forays over the SR Western Division main line in June 1948, Rebuilt Scot 4-6-0 No 46154 The Hussar *eases the down 'Atlantic Coast Express' out of Waterloo. For their SR trials both the Scot and the Stanier Pacific were temporarily paired with WD 2-8-0 tenders (specially lettered LMS for the occasion) to afford the engines extra water supplies in view of the SR's lack of water troughs.*

Class A4 Pacific No 22 Mallard *alongside an SR Lord Nelson 4-6-0 at Nine Elms shed during the 1948 Locomotive Exchanges.* Mallard *blotted its record by twice succumbing to middle big-end failures during the trials, once on the WR and once on the SR.*

Off their home ground the Bulleid Pacific participants in the 1948 Exchanges were temporarily paired with LM high-sided tenders to enable them to pick up from water troughs. The Merchant Navy officially tested on the 7.50 a.m. Leeds-Kings Cross with dynamometer car was No 35017, but No 35019 *French Line CGT,* one of a quartet specially prepared by Eastleigh for the event – the others were Nos 35018/20 – was sent over to make one of the preliminary trips, on which it is seen climbing from Beeston to Ardsley. The second coach of the train appears to be an ECJS clerestory.

Class A4 4-6-2 No 22 Mallard, *with GWR dynamometer car marshalled behind the tender, lifts the 'Atlantic Coast Express' out of Waterloo on its official test of 8 June 1948. In those days the 'ACE' timing to Salisbury was easy – 103 minutes for 83.8 miles – but the 500-ton train was a much tougher assignment over the hills beyond to Exeter; on this run Mallard cut the schedule to the Sidmouth Junction stop by 10¼ minutes.*

149

Three-cylinder Class N1 2-6-0 No 1879 toils up Hildenborough bank with a London-bound Eastern Section freight shortly after the war.

Class E 4-4-0 No 1491 on Hildenborough bank with an up train of the early post-war period that has the look of a returning hoppickers' special.

By the end of the last war all the Nelsons were based at Nine Elms, where No 863 was captured in close-up, restored from wartime black to malachite green, shortly before nationalisation.

Dover shed yard in the 1950s, with Bulleid Class Q1 0-6-0 No 33016 of Eastleigh shed, a somewhat unexpected sight alongside local Class N 2-6-0 No 31819.

151

Bulleid had the Schools 4-4-0s divested of their wartime black and returned to malachite green as quickly as possible after the end of the war. No 903 Charterhouse was one of the 25 which had been thus refurbished before nationalisation. One of the St Leonards shed allocation of nine Schools in the mid-1940s, it heads a Hastings train on Hildenborough bank, probably in 1947.

Still in wartime black livery, Class N15 4-6-0 No 784 Sir Nerovens accelerates away from Salisbury with a London train in the mid-1940s.

Overleaf:
The five-mile Horsted Keynes–Sheffield Park stretch of the SR line from East Grinstead to Lewes, the so-called 'Bluebell Railway', which was closed by BR in 1958 after determined but abortive legal efforts to frustrate abandonment, was the first British Railways standard-gauge line to be reopened by private enterprise. Heading a train of Bulleid corridor stock on the line is No 323 Bluebell, blue-liveried to suit its present name, but never styled that way in its public career: it was one of an 0-6-0T class built as push-pull light passenger engines for the South Eastern & Chatham Railway by Harry Wainwright in 1909, but in its final years employed by the SR chiefly as a light shunter.

Facing page:
Another of the present-day Bluebell Railway's treasures, ex-SECR Class C 0-6-0 No 592, restored to SECR livery with polished dome. Between 1900 and 1908 a total of 106 Class C 0-6-0s were constructed and the last pair, of which this was one, did not cease BR service until 1967.

152

OVER THE FELLS TO PENRITH

Had Britain not been spurred by its Industrial Revolution to pioneer the steam railway, quite likely Eric Treacy and a countless host of other photographers would have been denied one of the world's best-known settings for inspiring steam action, the last $4\frac{3}{4}$ miles of 1 in 75 to the 915ft shoulder of Shap Summit. Supposing the Central Europeans had been the front-runners and the Austrians had embarked earlier on the first transalpine tunnel, the Semmering, then the promoters of the Lancaster & Carlisle Railway might have had the courage to tunnel through the Lakeland mountains and spare enginemen that fierce grind up the open fellside.

Shap's aggravations have not ended with steam. In good weather Class 86 and 87 electrics sail easily up the slope, so much so that they may have to brake for the speed restriction at the summit. But their adhesion is put to critical test when conditions are bad. Then even the APT's wheel-slip warning lights on its driver's console are prone to flicker. And pending BR's acquisition of a Co-Co electric locomotive class, all Freightliners of more than 900 tons have to be double-headed up the hill.

Joseph Locke, who engineered the line, had plumped for the Shap Fell route when he was first bidden in 1835 by the Grand Junction Railway directors (at the time Locke's only appointment was that of GJR engineer) to prospect a possible route from Preston to Carlisle. 'I found', Locke reported, 'that without incurring any greater rise than 1 in 100 the summit at Shap Fell might be passed with a tunnel a little more than $1\frac{1}{4}$ miles.' Locke then envisaged following the Lune Valley from Lancaster, not the present route via Carnforth and Oxenholme. He would have kept company with the river through Kirkby Lonsdale, passing just to the west of Sedbergh, and rejoined the ultimate route at Low Gill. That way, he reckoned, the ascent to the summit from the south would have been tamed to $4\frac{1}{2}$ miles of 1 in 140, then $3\frac{1}{2}$ miles of 1 in 100 and a final $1\frac{1}{4}$ miles of 1 in 260 in the summit tunnel. The northern ramp would be $7\frac{1}{4}$ miles of continuous 1 in 165.

The Lune Valley plan soon came under withering fire. Locke and the GJR may have had their sights on the supreme goal of an Anglo-Scottish rail link and its achievement by the shortest feasible route, but the citizenry of England's north-west corner were far more concerned that the railway should serve their doorsteps. Kendal, for one, was outraged at its neglect, especially as Locke had stressed the town's importance in his preliminary report. The mining and

On Sunday 31 August 1975 a total of 34 preserved steam locomotives were mobilised at Shildon to celebrate the 150th anniversary of the Stockton & Darlington Railway opening. As they were prepared for the parade at BR's Shildon Wagon Works 'enthusiasts of every age were tending their engines like stable lads at Newmarket', Eric Treacy wrote at the time.
'When they were not polishing they were photographing, and the dirtier the job, the happier they were. Both sexes too. There were comely young maidens burnishing buffers and godly matrons brewing tea for their male attachments.' With steam up and ready to go is GWR 57XX class 0-6-0PT No 7752 from Tyseley; behind is GWR 4-6-0 No 6960.

157

industrial interests in West Cumberland, too, agitated for consideration of a circuitous route via Furness and Maryport.

The West Cumbrians enlisted the advice of George Stephenson, who had fallen out with Locke during the GJR's construction. Stephenson expectedly criticised the Locke plan, forecasting that the Shap route would be unusably blocked by snow for weeks at a time every winter, though he was not as scathing as some subsequent accounts have alleged; it was his West Cumbrian sponsors, not Stephenson, who broadcast dire warnings that Locke's long gradients would encourage such speed that on the curves 'the danger of precipitating the whole train into the glen below would be imminent'. Not too far-fetched a vision, perhaps, when the only brakes on trains in those primitive times were on engine and brake-van.

Stephenson advocated a route which was ultimately built as the first member of the later Furness Railway, except that he suggested a much shorter cut across Morecambe Bay, by a curved embankment from Poulton-le-Sands. A few years later, in 1838, his scheme was elaborated for the West Cumbrians by John Hague, who conceived an even more direct crossing of Morecambe Bay, on a causeway no less than $10\frac{5}{8}$ miles long, which would have absorbed almost $10\frac{1}{2}$ million tons of material. But even so the rail distance from Lancaster to Carlisle via Whitehaven would have been about 96 miles, compared with the 67 miles of the Lune Valley scheme.

The leading citizens of Kendal and Penrith, meanwhile, had mobilised a local man of considerable talent, John Bintley, who combined really professional skills as a surveyor with management of a prosperous drapery business, to investigate a third possible route. It would take in Carnforth and Kendal, then follow Longsleddale and the west bank of Hawes Water. To get from the dale to the lake Bintley proposed a $2\frac{1}{4}$-mile tunnel under Gatescarth.

Bintley's would have been a more easily graded line than Locke's Lune Valley route and also two miles shorter. But the tunnel construction would have entailed sinking working shafts of then unprecedented depth, one of them dropping as much as 824ft, and with railway tunnelling still in its infancy that was a serious deterrent to the Commissioners which Parliament appointed to adjudicate on the rival Lancaster-to-Carlisle proposals in 1838.

The Commissioners advocated Locke's Lune Valley route, but they sowed the seeds of the ultimate product by suggesting that some compromise of the Kendal and Shap schemes would repay study. At that the Kendal faction initiated a fresh survey, which established the feasibility of cutting across from their area to the Lune Valley at Low Gill via Grayrigg. However, it would mean sacrificing direct main-line service of Kendal; the new surveyor, George Larmer, had to agree with Locke that there was no way of driving a railway out of the town to Shap on an acceptable gradient, and that Oxenholme must be Kendal's nearest main-line railhead.

The Commissioners duly approved the Grayrigg route to Tebay

in 1841. Beyond Tebay both Larmer and Locke were now minded to avoid the Shap summit and detour to the east, with a tunnel under Orton Scar, but a reversion to the original path over Shap and agreement on the present descent from the summit through Thrimby Grange and Clifton to Penrith seems to have been dictated by the hardnosed attitude of the Grand Junction Railway, which had a substantial stake in the embryonic Lancaster & Carlisle Railway, and by the latter's trouble in raising local cash too.

The picaresque Mark Huish, representing the GJR at the first Carlisle meeting called to consider the formation of a Lancaster & Carlisle Railway company, insisted that economy be a paramount concern of its builders. 'They must be satisfied to go over the hills, not through them,' he said. So a compliant Locke scrapped as much of the earthworks in his original scheme as he could and ran the eventual railway up to the summit in the open at a continuous 1 in 75.

In 1898 the LNWR obtained Parliamentary powers for a deviation to the west, starting just north of Tebay in the vicinity of Loups Fell, keeping closer to the course of the Birk Beck, diving into tunnel for about a mile and rejoining the historic route between Shap summit and Shap station. This 8.9-mile bypass would have held the ruling gradient to 1 in 135. Having won its powers, however, the LNWR never exercised them. According to one source, the LMS had them renewed in one of its 1930s Acts, but I have been unable to verify this.

Of course, the Lune Valley did eventually get a railway, the Ingleton–Low Gill branch. This was the line on which the LNWR and the Midland crossed swords. It was the concept of the so-called 'Little North Western', but in the aftermath of the Railway Mania's collapse that concern had been forced to rein in and content itself with a single-line branch from Clapham, on what was to become its Skipton–Morecambe main line, to Ingleton. The Midland took over in 1852, at first on a 21-year lease, and immediately took up the Ingleton–Low Gill project, keen to shorten the journeys of its Scottish passengers and transfer them to the Lancaster & Carlisle at Low Gill instead of Lancaster.

But in 1859 the LNWR took over the Lancaster & Carlisle. Already alarmed at the Midland's erosion of its traffic further south, the LNWR was not about to ease the Midland into the Anglo-Scottish market. Rather than allow the Midland to fill the Low Gill–Ingleton gap, it hurried to lay its own double-track branch, over which it could not only impose its own operating restrictions but take financial toll of every Midland train trying to crack the Scottish business. For years it refused to let the Midland run so much as a through coach beyond Tebay, which drove the frustrated Midland to plan its own trans-Pennine route to Carlisle via Ais Gill.

In the 20th century LNWR and Midland relations were more amicable. From the summer of 1910 until the first world war the

159

10 a.m. from Leeds to Scotland and the 10.30 Edinburgh–Leeds were routed via the Ingleton–Low Gill branch and Penrith instead of over Ais Gill. At the same time connections between Midland and LNWR trains throughout the area were cooperatively improved. By connection with the 10.30 from Edinburgh at Penrith, for instance, a traveller from Keswick could make St Pancras within 6 hours 40 minutes. At this period the two companies also combined in a summer through train working between Leeds and Keswick.

Sedbergh was the only town of any commercial significance on the Ingleton–Low Gill branch. That numbered only about 2,500 inhabitants, besides which its station was a mile out of the town, so unsurprisingly the line's passenger service was in jeopardy as soon as motoring became commonplace in the 1930s. But the branch clung to its local trains until February 1954, because the unified LMS and for some nationalisation years its London Midland Region successor valued it as a bypass in the event of a crisis between Preston and Tebay on the West Coast main line. Then even Stanier Pacifics were allowed to take the deviation.

In the late 1930s, when Eric Treacy began to play his camera over the fells, one could catch some piquant motive power contrasts. At Tebay and Penrith Stanier's latest streamlined Pacifics could cast their shadows not only over ex-LNWR passenger tanks and 'Cauliflower' 0-6-0s, but over Great Eastern 2-4-0s.

In the autumn of 1935 the LNER despatched six ex-GE Class E4 2-4-0s north for distribution between Darlington, Kirkby Stephen, Penrith, Barnard Castle and Middleton-in-Teesdale sheds. At the time it was exercised to find suitable traction for its viciously graded trans-Pennine line from Darlington to Penrith and Tebay. The ex-NER Class D23 4-4-0s employed in the early 1930s were extinct, some ex-GN Class D3 4-4-0s sent to replace them were winded by the long banks and local enginemen were mishandling the ex-NER Class J21 0-6-0s. With driving wheels no bigger than 5ft 8in the E4 2-4-0s seem to have been the best bet until drivers got the hang of working the J21s without breaking them.

Both 4-4-2 and 4-6-2 ex-LNW tanks were plying the Cockermouth, Keswick & Penrith line and the Ingleton–Low Gill branch in the 1930s. On the CK&P line they were required in summer to wear express headlamps, for its seasonal traffic included through trains to Keswick both from the North-East and from Euston. The latter was a section of a train embracing all the Lakeland branches which the LMS named the 'Lakes Express' in 1927.

The 'Lakes Express', the 12 noon out of Euston in the 1930s, was in those days a multi-section train of almost Continental complexity. Non-stop from Rugby to Wigan on a near mile-a-minute timing, it dropped at its first Lancashire stop a two-coach Blackpool portion (which on the return journey was picked up at Preston). At Lancaster two more coaches were put off to take the coast route via Barrow to Whitehaven, Workington and Maryport; there was no balancing up

OVER THE FELLS TO PENRITH

working of this section. The core of the train, including its three-coach restaurant-kitchen set, took the Windermere branch from Oxenholme. And the residual three coaches were then taken on to Penrith for reversal up the branch to Keswick on a CK&P train.

At some stage a comprehensive bridge-strengthening programme was ordered in anticipation of a rising graph of railborne Lakeland tourism, for in the immediate post-war years power as bulky as a Rebuilt Scot 4-6-0 was licensed to work from Penrith to Keswick. That was on a summer Sunday through buffet car train from Newcastle via Carlisle which had no need to reverse at Penrith. The train's customary traction, however, was a pair of 'Black Five' 4-6-0s.

As for the 'Lakes Express', for a period that became one of the West Coast main line's heaviest trains. In a rather unfathomable timetable revision which detached the Barrow/Whitehaven portion at Crewe and had it tail the main train as far as Lancaster, with identical stops at Wigan and Preston, both parts were furnished with separate restaurant-kitchen facilities.

But Beeching put a stop to such extravagance. The summer of 1965 was the curtain call for the 'Lakes Express'. The following spring the CK&P's passenger service was killed off west of Keswick. And the bitterly controversial abandonment even of the dmu operation between Penrith and Keswick was finally achieved in March 1972.

The Keswick section of the up 'Lakes
Express' is at the rear of this 1930s train
near Eden Valley Junction behind
Precursor ex-LNW 4-4-2T No 6824.

Ex-GE Class E4 2-4-0 No 7416 of the
LNER leaves Penrith with a string of three
ex-NER clerestories, heading for the trans-
Pennine line to Darlington.

A 1930s freight heads away from Carlisle
for the fells behind ex-LNW 0-8-0 No 9120.

A Carlisle Canal Class 2P 4-4-0, No 652, is mobilised to assist Jubilee 4-6-0 No 5720 Indomitable *south with an early post-war Edinburgh–Liverpool train; the pair are pulling out of Penrith on 7 September 1946.*

Heading south, rebuilt Royal Scot 4-6-0 No 46121 Highland Light Infantry, City of Glasgow Regiment (*it was more compactly named H.L.I. in LMS days) overfills its tanks on Dillicar troughs.*

Carlisle Canal Jubilee 4-6-0 No 5688 Polyphemus *restarts a southbound semi-fast from Penrith in the late 1930s.*

Round about the late 1930s ex-LNW Class
2F 'Cauliflower' 0-6-0 No 8499 of
Workington shed huffs away from Penrith
with a Keswick–Workington branch train.

A Class 4 2-6-4T from Carnforth shed, No
42601, bustles up the bank to Shap at
Greenholme with an all-stations train to
Penrith in the days before diesel multiple-
units and Beeching.

Final chapter on the Cockermouth Keswick
& Penrith branch: a dmu at Threlkeld.

One of the unnamed Patriot 4-6-0s, No 45542, a mile out from Tebay, labours up the bank to Shap at Greenholme with a northbound freight, helped in the rear by a 2-6-4T.

In the first year of nationalisation, with the train still in LMS livery and with Pacific No 46210 Lady Patricia still in wartime black, the morning Birmingham–Glasgow approaches Shap Summit. The picture was taken with the Zeiss Contessa Press camera which Eric Treacy bought in 1936, but which he nearly parted with in 1939 because he was unhappy at the results he obtained from it.

In 1951–3 three Class A1 Pacifics, Nos 60152/60/1, were shedded at Glasgow Polmadie for comparison with Stanier Pacifics on the route south to England. On one turn they worked only as far as Carlisle, but they also covered a lodging turn to Crewe on the up 'West Coast Postal' and the morning Birmingham–Glasgow train back, with which No 60161 North British is climbing to Shap Summit.

A Glasgow Fair Saturday extra to the south leaves the Lune Valley at Low Gill behind BR Class 6 Pacific No 72003 Clan Fraser.

The clouds dapple the hillsides as 'Crab' 2-6-0 No 42786 passes Low Gill and leads its northbound freight into the Lune Gorge.

Another wartime Euston–Glasgow express, the 16-car 'Royal Scot' (note the absence of restaurant cars), on the final grind up to Shap Summit, headed by Stanier Pacific No 6230 Duchess of Buccleuch, as yet without smoke deflectors.

Facing page:
A Class 27 approaches the highest summit on the West Highland line, between Bridge of Orchy and Tyndrum, with a train from Fort William to Glasgow.

Overleaf:
One of the 13 preserved Class 5 4-6-0s, No 45407 poses by the coaling plant at Steamtown, Carnforth. Another of the type, No 5428, has been named Eric Treacy by its owners. The Class 5s were the mainstay of the Kyle line in the latter years of steam.

ROADS TO THE ISLES

In the steam era far more purple prose was lavished on the West Highland road to Scotland's Western Isles than on the Kyle line. But not with total justification. Granted, the Kyle line never gave one so continuous an impression of puny human invention matched against the eternal, aloof mountains as the West Highland did, but the Kyle line had its spectacular stretches. Arguably it traversed an area of much wilder beauty.

Until Stanier and BR standard Class 5s invaded the West Highland, there was certainly more individuality about the ex-LNER route's motive power, with its mixture of 2-6-0s and from time to time the two Gresley Class V4 2-6-2s, *Bantam Cock* and her sister. They would probably have procreated as the LNER's equivalent of the LMS and GWR mixed traffic 4-6-0 had Gresley lived longer and his successor not discarded the design in favour of his B1 4-6-0s.

But even in the 1950s the Kyle line had its engaging operational and equipment idiosyncrasies. Travelling on the morning train from Inverness, for instance, you would start out with one of the old flat-roofed Highland mail vans at the head of the train. Quite why was unfathomable, as it was detached at Dingwall, there to be picked up shortly afterwards by the following Inverness–Wick train for onward movement to its destination at Helmsdale. On its return the mail van was subjected to the same strange sojourn at Dingwall, in that direction for some 4½ hours, before it resumed its journey to Inverness, but a Kyle train was not involved in the last part of the southbound movement.

At the outset of the 1950s you would probably take your lunch on the morning Kyle train in an ex-L&Y 12-wheeled kitchen restaurant car. And when that was retired, its successor could well be one of the aged Clayton Pullmans inherited by BR as a result of the 1934 LMS acquisition of the cars operated on the Caledonian by the Pullman Car Company. BR ran them long enough to repaint them first in crimson-and-cream and then in maroon. By the mid-1950s, however, the operators did their best to keep the Pullmans on the Wick rather than the Kyle line, because the latter's sharp curves made the Clayton cars unruly riders.

The climax of lunch and of the Kyle trip coincided, as the 'Black Five', the Kyle line's staple power after 1948, tackled the 15-mile grind up to the 646ft-high Luib summit, much of it as steep as 1 in 60/75 and with the ruling slope a gruelling 1 in 40. Almost always, moreover, the engine would be contending with a fierce headwind

A pair of Class 25 diesels bring a Highland line train into Dalnaspidal station.

A pair of Class 25s at Inverness, butting up to a ramp used for loading cars on to Motorail services.

177

howling through the wild Strath Braan and around the gaunt cone of the 2,778ft Scuir Villin, dominating the landscape to the left of the train. Gaunt mountains dwarfed the pygmy train plodding through a landscape barren of life or habitation, except where the valley floor broadened into an oasis of dark fir trees surrounding the Achanalt passing loop.

At Achanalt you would be chivvied to finish your post-prandial coffee, for at the next stop, Achnasheen, the restaurant car was switched to the up morning train from Kyle, though you would never have believed it from the public timetable, which showed the up train departing before the down train's arrival. That covered the exigencies of the manœuvring, not only to transfer the diner, but also to process three trains at once through the plain passing loop at Achnasheen.

The down train was preceded into the down platform by the morning freight from Kyle. Next to arrive was the up passenger train, which transacted its business, then drew up to the eastern extremity of the up loop to allow the freight to clear the down platform and back in behind it, brake to brake. Now the down passenger train could be admitted to the down platform, whereafter the up passenger train's engine detached itself, coupled on to the diner at the rear of the down train, transferred it to the front of the Inverness-bound train and immediately resumed its journey eastward. Today's attraction of an observation car on the summer 10.35 Inverness–Kyle is not really adequate compensation for the loss of such charming eccentricities.

On the ex-LNER West Highland Line, Class K2 2-6-0 No 61787 Loch Quoich leaves Fort William with a Mallaig train in the early 1950s.

Through the beautiful Monessie Gorge, between Roy Bridge and Tulloch, an up West Highland freight is headed by Class K4 2-6-0 No 61996 Lord of the Isles. The three-cylinder K4 was Gresley's 1937 response to the demand for an engine with 50 per cent more tractive effort than the earlier K2 2-6-0, but one that would at the same time satisfy the West Highland's stringent bridge loading limits, so as to reduce the double-heading of summer West Highland trains steadily increasing in weight through rising traffic demand for sleeper service.

Stanier Class 5 4-6-0 No 45098 brings the morning Kyle goods from Dingwall into Achnasheen in the 1950s. Note the vintage clerestory-roofed sleeper doing duty as a goods office on the left. Despite its bleak and lonely situation, Achnasheen is an important railhead for road traffic from Loch Maree, Glen Torridon and Gairloch to the north-west.

A general view of Kyle of Lochalsh, with 'Black Five' 4-6-0 No 45453 at the platform. Despite the fact that the working timetable graded them as Class B stopping trains, the LMS considered that two of the Kyle line trains merited names. The morning mail from Inverness and the crack-of-dawn 5.05 a.m. from Kyle were the 'Lewisman'. The up 'Lewisman' was probably the only regular British titled train of the 20th century with no refreshment service (famished passengers had to wait until arrival at Inverness for breakfast). The main mid-morning departures from Inverness and Kyle were branded the 'Hebridean'.

Ex-Caledonian 0-4-4T No 55216 shunts at Kyle of Lochalsh. Alongside, a Class 5 4-6-0 pulls out to pass through the narrow rock cutting at the neck of the station.

PENNINE PROSPECTS

It was the confrontation of Pacifics, Scots and Jubilees at Leeds and the toil of trains heading for the 'Long Drag' that chiefly absorbed Eric Treacy's camera during his spells at Keighley and Halifax, but a prospect of one of Yorkshire's most entertaining trunk routes was within walking distance of his Halifax Vicarage. From the cliff face on the town's outskirts popularly known as The Rocks, with its curious embellishment of an ornamental mill chimney, a folly called the Wainhouse Tower, one commanded a view of a corner of the Calder Valley main line's triangular junction with the route to Halifax, Low Moor and Bradford.

In the mid-1950s the Lancashire & Yorkshire Railway ambience of the route was far from dispelled. One could even have recollections of the L&YR's prime stirred by the regular sight of one of its 2-4-2 tanks sporting an express passenger headcode, though on pilot and not train engine duty. The 'South Yorkshireman' from Marylebone, re-routed via Halifax between Huddersfield and Bradford from the summer of 1953, was deemed to need help up the 1 in 120 from the Calder Valley's Greetland Junction into Halifax, so its Low Moor Class 5 4-6-0 was given the assistance from Huddersfield of the engine off an evening Bradford–Huddersfield local, and that was normally a 2-4-2T.

By this time Riddles WD 2-8-0s commanded most of the main line coal hauls, but ex-L&Y 0-6-0s still pottered about the branches and clung to some of the through traffic. Several were shedded almost within sight of The Rocks, at Sowerby Bridge to the west, where half-a-dozen Fowler 0-8-0s also survived to relieve the monotonous parade of Austerities. The town had lost its Rishworth branch service, once furnished by an L&Y steam rail-motor, way back in 1929, but in the mid-1950s it was still the turnround point of some local passenger trains from both Wakefield and Bradford, for which the local shed deployed a small stud of 2-6-4 tanks. On summer Saturdays, too, it originated a scheduled through train to Scarborough.

Aside from its rather curious layout, with a down relief line enclosed by platform faces, Sowerby Bridge station claims some indirect distinction in the realm of letters. Distinction is possibly an inapt word, since the link is the egregious Bramwell Brontë, who doused his artistic potential in drink. Taking up railway service as a last resort, Bramwell became the new Sowerby Bridge station's first booking clerk. He applied himself to that job with enough sobriety to be appointed stationmaster at neighbouring Luddendenfoot, but in 1842 he was abruptly dismissed for negligence. From then on, to the horror of his sisters, he steadily drank himself to death.

The Hughes Lancashire & Yorkshire 'Dreadnought' 4-6-0 which is included among the Pennine scenes was probably captured in 1938. A year earlier only a sanguine betting man would have laid money on the survival of any of the class to be photographed the following summer.

Under Fowler during the late 1920s the LMS had been pretty indulgent of a class that notoriously gobbled coal, was a temperamental steamer and a nightmare to keep in steamtight order, and which could give its crews a sickmaking ride. However, with the new Group's only other four-cylinder 4-6-0s, the ex-LNWR Claughtons, just as bitterly criticised under some of these heads, the range of alternatives was limited. Between Grouping and 1932 the LMS discarded only five of the 75-strong Hughes 4-6-0 class.

But with the start of successful Claughton rebuilding, then the mass production of Stanier's Jubilee and Class 5 4-6-0s, the Hughes engines were marked off as a costly extravagance. A holocaust was ordered that abruptly disposed of 59 of them between 1933 and mid-1937.

Then, inexplicably, the massacre was not merely halted but the remaining 4-6-0s were given a purposeful extension of life. The 11 survivors were taken into works, given new copper fireboxes and tubes, fitted with the latest type of lubricators in place of their original Wakefield mechanical devices, and decked out in the full regalia of LMS lined crimson lake livery. Up to the outbreak of the second world war only one more had been put to the torch and six lasted to become BR property. One of these even clung to life long enough to assume BR lined black livery and a BR number, 50455, in the spring of 1949; it was honoured with one of the first swan-song excursions for railway enthusiasts, which it powered from Blackpool to York and back via Manchester on 1 July 1951, though it was not officially condemned until the following October.

The first 20 Hughes 4-6-0s emerged in 1908-9. They were a dramatic departure from the Aspinall lineage of Lancashire & Yorkshire express passenger power, which was characterised by inside cylinders and big driving wheels of no less than 7ft 3in diameter in his graceful 'Highflyer' Atlantics. The Hughes' 4-6-0s' driving wheels were no larger than 6ft 3in, and they were four-cylinder engines. Sadly, their aggressive mien was belied by unadventurous design that eschewed superheating and had all four cylinders fitted with slide valves actuated by Joy, not Walschaerts valve gear. Consequently, on the turns where their extra punch compared with the Aspinall engines was really needed – on some of the York runs with Liverpool–Newcastle trains and on the heaviest Liverpool–Manchester jobs, where the L&YR had to compete with the LNWR and CLC parallel services on the same 40-minute schedule despite the longest (36.4 miles) and most viciously graded route of the three – the Hughes

183

One of the 11 Hughes 'Dreadnought' 4-6-0s refurbished and accorded lined LMS crimson lake livery in 1937, No 10412, is caught at Euxton Junction on a Preston-Manchester stopping train. In the last two pre-war years Blackpool shed used the Hughes engines on all its top-link jobs, including the morning and evening 'Club Trains' to and from Manchester, for which the LMS provided two palatial saloons to sustain a facility to which the L&YR had first agreed in 1895; the special accommodation, including attendant service of refreshments, for businessmen living on the coast was in exchange for guaranteed purchase of a specific number of annual season ticket sales at a premium rate.

4-6-0s could only deliver at an exorbitant cost in coal. E. S. Cox has written that he never came across a higher rate of consumption per drawbar-horsepower-hour in his whole career. Besides which, as already remarked, much of the engines' detail design made their maintenance purgatorial.

Hughes recognised the flaws in the 4-6-0s and might have tackled them earlier but for first world war preoccupations. At last, in 1920–1, he had 15 rebuilt with superheaters, piston valves and separate Walschaerts gear for each cylinder. Fortified by the results he put 35 more engines with these modifications into production in 1921, and a final 20 were built in 1924–5, after Hughes had been appointed the first LMS Chief Mechanical Engineer. This concluding score were actually laid down as 4-6-4 tanks, but Hughes stopped construction of that type which he had set out to make the LMS standard short-haul passenger machine after only 10 had been completed, concluding that the operational need of tender engines was the more urgent; however, 20 more had been started, so their frames were cropped to turn them into tender 4-6-0s.

These last 20 engines were shedded on the Western Division of the LMS, chiefly at Carlisle Upperby, and until the advent of the Fowler Royal Scots shared the West Coast main line express working north of Crewe with ex-LNWR 4-6-0s. On occasions the Hughes engines reached as far as Euston.

After the inexplicable reprieve of the last 11 Hughes 4-6-0s in mid-1937, they were massed at Blackpool, which was to be their final base. Until the outbreak of war they were used turn and turn about with Jubilees and 'Black Fives' on the shed's top-link jobs, but as the war progressed they were demoted. All were eventually clad in wartime black livery. By 1945 most were out of use, but in the late 1940s Blackpool reconditioned them for two or three years' more service.

Another scene south of Preston station just before the last war: one of Aspinall's L&Y 0-6-0s, No 12619 of the LMS, trundles freight southward.

One of Sowerby Bridge's Fowler 0-8-0s, No 49674, threads the Calder Valley near Luddendenfoot with coal empties returning to the Yorkshire pits. After the last war the class had been massed on the Central Division of the LMS, where engine-crews invariably dubbed them the 'Austin Sevens'. Because of a poorly designed chassis they were costly to maintain and all were withdrawn between 1959 and 1962.

Sowerby Bridge station looking east towards Halifax; the Wainhouse Tower, referred to in the preceding text, is conspicuous on the left-hand horizon. Class 5 4-6-0 No 44694 approaches the station on a York–Manchester train, passing an ex-L&Y 0-6-0 and 2-4-2T on the local shed.

Early in the 1960s a Fowler 2-6-4T from Leeds Neville Hill shed, No 42384, leaves Huddersfield with a local train for Clayton West.

EDINBURGH AND THE 'ELIZABETHAN'

Edinburgh and its environs were one of Eric Treacy's favourite settings. And year after year the centre of his stage was taken by the Kings Cross–Edinburgh non-stop.

One tends to forget that the steam speed title was not the only global distinction Gresley's Pacifics held to the end of the steam age. They had no rivals either for their 392.8 miles daily non-stop stint each summer timetable season on the East Coast main line. Except for an inevitable hiatus during the last war and its aftermath, the Gresley engines monopolised the job from 1928 to 1961, the non-streamlined Pacifics until 1936, the A4s thereafter. Admittedly, no one advanced any performance reason why the Peppercorn A1s could not have shared the non-stop duty in the 1950s; all that debarred them was a technical practicality, the incompatibility of the vacuum-braked Gresley corridor tenders with the post-war class, which was built with steam-braked tenders.

It was initially the 'Flying Scotsman' train which resumed the summer non-stop speciality, in 1948. Now, more than 30 years later, it seems scarcely credible, even with due allowance for the infrastructure improvements of the 1960s and 1970s, that the operators felt they had to cosset the A4s with an end-to-end timing of 7 hours 50 minutes, over three hours more than the book requires of the present-day Inter-City 125 'Flying Scotsman'.

As it happened, the non-stop needed a good deal more time for about half its first post-war season. In the second week of August 1949 the whole littoral from the Forth to the Tweed was swamped with six days' unbroken rain. The East Coast main line was ripped apart and undermined so catastrophically that the havoc took eleven weeks even to patch up with temporary, speed-restricted bridges, and for much of that period the non-stop 'Scotsman' made a fresh mark in the annals.

In the first week it was diverted via Carlisle, for the last two days via Selby Canal and Gascoigne Wood to Leeds City, not via Newcastle (the 'Queen of Scots' was re-directed the same way). The up train's power over Ais Gill was not recorded, but the down train's was: a Midland Class 2P 4-4-0 and a 'Black Five' 4-6-0 in double harness on the first day, and on the second A4 Pacific No 25 *Falcon*, very likely the first of its type to negotiate the Settle & Carlisle line.

By the end of that first week the engineers had put the Border branches to rights, so the 'Scotsman' could now turn off the Waverley Route at St Boswells and take the single line via Kelso back to the main line at Tweedmouth. That cut the Edinburgh–Kings Cross distance to 408.7 miles, only about 16 miles more than the 'Scotsman's' normal course. But resumption of non-stop working seemed inconceivable, seeing that the detour confronted the A4 with a 7½-mile grind at a ruling 1 in 70 up to the 900ft Falahill summit, in the rift dividing the Lammermuir and Moorfoot hills; besides the single line was studded with permanent speed restrictions from which the A4 would have to recover speed and thereby expend more abnormal effort. In fact, the operators prudently tabled an operational stop at Galashiels so that the A4's crew could top up their tender, since a Pacific taking the East Coast main line customarily used up half its 5,000 gallons between leaving Waverley and refilling on Lucker troughs, south of Tweedmouth; an assistant engine was also posted ready for the 'Scotsman' at Galashiels.

But the Haymarket shed Top Link of the period numbered some enterprising characters who did not drive by the union rulebook, and who eagerly grabbed the chance to probe the ultimate capacity of their mounts. When things were normal these men frequently ignored Lucker troughs and drew no fresh water until they stopped at Newcastle. The very first day of new routeing via the Border branches, Driver Stevenson on No 60028 spurned the stop at Galashiels and kept his train continuously moving until the exchange with the Kings Cross crew via the corridor tender between Darlington and York. After that first non-stop run over the extended distance, other Haymarket crews responded to the challenge to the extent that eight more southbound and eight northbound truly non-stop 'Scotsman' runs over the taxing 408.7-mile course were recorded before the end of the season.

The following summer, 1949, the East Coast regions decided that the resurgent peacetime traffic justified a couple of morning Anglo-Scottish trains each way. The 'Flying Scotsman' was bidden to continue its winter calls at Grantham and Newcastle, and a new train was created at 9.30 from Kings Cross and 9.45 from Edinburgh to perform the summer non-stop working. Initially it was titled the 'Capitals Limited', and because the main line was still not completely free of speed limits over the flood-ravaged sector north of the Border its overall timing was a depressing eight hours.

The 'Capitals Limited' commandeered the pressure-ventilated Thompson train-sets built for the 'Scotsman' in 1947, each complete with buffet-lounge as well as a three-car restaurant set and with the frill of a ladies' settee-furnished retiring-room. So much of the 13-car, 473 tons-tare formation was pre-empted by this non-revenue-earning accommodation, however, and also by the generally super-fluous full brake which seems to have been included purely to pre-serve an unadultered Thompson line (no brake firsts had featured in the 'Scotsman' building programme) that first-class seats were always at a premium in the 'Capitals Limited'. There were only eight first-class compartments in the whole train, a ludicrously meagre provi-

189

sion for such a prestige service, and three of those were in the Aberdeen section which the 'Capitals' took over from the 'Scotsman' for the summer. The first-class clientele got a steadily worse deal as the load was curtailed to allow schedule cutting. By 1952, when it had been trimmed to 11 cars and the timing to 7 hours 6 minutes, first-class accommodation was down to a mere 42 compartment seats plus 18 in the saloon of a kitchen-restaurant car.

The zenith of the non-stop working was 1955–6. The train had been re-titled the 'Elizabethan' in 1953 to mark the present Queen's Coronation and quickened to a $6\frac{3}{4}$-hour schedule, the first time that the pre-war non-stop timing had been improved upon. The following year the allowance was screwed up to $6\frac{1}{2}$ hours and that was never surpassed; it was in fact eased by five minutes for the concluding four years of the non-stop's career, from 1957 to 1961. The non-stop's performance in 1954 was fallible, partly because the A4s, still three years away from the wretchedly belated fitting of the whole class with Kylchap double blastpipes and chimneys which so strikingly rejuvenated them, were feeling their years, partly because the civil engineers were plastering the East Coast main line with possessions. But in 1955 the A4s were on better form and less shackled by the civils' harassments; on at least one occasion a non-stop run came within five minutes of the pre-war 'Coronation' streamliner's six-hour booking on a net reckoning that excluded time sacrificed to signal and other checks.

Both Haymarket and Kings Cross sheds picked their A4s for summer non-stop duty in time for the engines to get an unscheduled overhaul at Doncaster before the start of the season. Reliable steaming rather than overheating of the notorious Gresley middle big-end was the preoccupation in the mid-1950s and that naturally prompted Kings Cross to prefer the three of the four A4s built with Kylchap double chimney and blastpipe which it had on its allocation, Nos 60022/33/4 (the fourth, No 60005, was a Gateshead engine). After 1951, the crack Kings Cross A4s were permanently allocated to a pair of crews, a practice which Haymarket had adopted at an earlier post-war date and the benefit of which was invariably patent in the superb external condition of the Edinburgh shed's Pacifics; more often than not their cab fitments were splendidly burnished too. Kings Cross always nominated a spare non-stop engine each summer weekday and ensured that it was reserved to short-haul jobs, so that the London shed would be certain of recovering it the same day for fresh standby duty at 'Elizabethan' departure time next morning.

No 60068 Sir Visto *was another Class A3 Pacific which spent practically the whole war and the rest of its peacetime years at Carlisle Canal shed; near the end of its career it starts the 'Waverley' from Edinburgh.*

With Arthur's Seat dominating the horizon, Class 55 No 9003 Meld *accelerates the up 'Afternoon Talisman' past Portobello East in the 1964 summer. This was the period of a misguided and brief assignment of Pullmans, made spare by the 'Queen of Scots' transmutation as the 'White Rose', to both 'Talisman' services as their only first-class accommodation; the rear, second-class cars had their own restaurant-buffet.*

194

Devoid of the train's headboard, Kings
Cross Class A4 Pacific No 60014 Silver
Link, *modified with double-chimney, lifts
the up 'Flying Scotsman' out of Edinburgh
Waverley at the close of the 1950s. The
engine name was derived from lines in
Walter Scott's* Lay of the Last Minstrel,
*which characterised true love as 'the silver
link, the silken tie, Which heart to heart
and mind to mind, In body and in soul can
bind'.*

195

Haymarket Class J38 0-6-0 No 65920
lumbers out of the tunnel east of
Edinburgh Waverley with a transfer
freight.

A Class V1 2-6-2T bustles off the Forth
Bridge and into Dalmeny station with a
stopping train from Thornton Junction to
Waverley.

THE CHARISMA OF CARLISLE

At Leeds the two sections of the City station paraded all the express passenger types of the East and West Coast regions bar the Stanier Pacifics, but at Carlisle they all congregated under the same roof; and Stanier Pacifics were there in profusion to exchange shadows with Doncaster's products, though admittedly an A4 was a rare arrival.

But in the 1950s the working of the station was as absorbing as the meeting of the locomotive giants. In those days the Waverley route was feeding trains into the station for the Midlands as well as the ex-Glasgow & South Western line from Glasgow St Enoch, and Beeching had yet to purge all the summer Saturday extras. When Glasgow Fair Week was on that alone could add as many as 55 trains to the Saturday timetable.

A high proportion of trains in each direction were booked to change engines at Carlisle. Besides that, the expresses would need as many of their toilet tanks as possible replenished during the Carlisle stop, which only the 'Royal Scot' spurned and that exclusively in the summer season, when it was nominally non-stop north of Crewe but paused outside Kingmoor shed going down to change crews and at Upperby shed coming south for the same purpose. Only three platforms were available to transact the through train business, which also included a great deal of parcels transfer. Any train passing Carlisle tended to attract packages for the whole of Scotland one way and almost any English destination the other. And only two of the three platforms were reversibly signalled.

So at the height of a summer Saturday each of these main platforms was in almost continuous occupation. The most noticeable pauses in activity occurred when the direction of working in one of the reversible platforms was altered, as the operators naturally endeavoured to 'flight' the trains each way and avoid alternating the use of platform by up and down services.

Activity around the Carlisle Kingmoor
turntable, with Camden Rebuilt Scot 4-6-0
No 46161 King's Own *in the foreground.*

Facing top:
A Barrow 'Black Five' 4-6-0, No 45386,
*eases a freight out of Upperby yard (the
shed is on the right). In the 1950s scarcely
any freight traversed Carlisle without being
tripped from one yard to another, work
which commanded the provision of 18
locomotives every weekday. London Road
yard served Newcastle line traffic, Petteril
Bridge the Leeds route, Upperby the West
Coast main line to the south, Currock the
West Cumberland lines, Canal the
Waverley route and Kingmoor exchange
traffic from Glasgow by either route, in
addition to which there were two yards
exclusively for local freight – Crown Street
and Bog.*

Facing bottom:
*One of the countless daily trip workings of
the 1950s between Carlisle's numerous
yards: ex-North British Class J36 0-6-0 No
65321 of the local Canal shed trundles a
line of loaded ore wagons past Carlisle
Kingmoor shed.*

In the autumn of 1958 the Midland main line was handed a number of Britannia Pacifics to release its Rebuilt Scot 4-6-0s to the LMR's Western Division. Among the intake were Scotland's Nos 70053/4 with Type BR1D 9-ton capacity tenders, of which No 70054 Dornoch Firth *heads the 'Thames-Clyde Express' out of Carlisle to Glasgow.*

In BR early experimental blue livery, former streamlined Pacific No 46221 Queen Elizabeth of Polmadie shed is about to start for home with the morning Birmingham-Glasgow express in 1952.

At the north end of the station, in No 7 platform, one of the two bays always used by Waverley route trains from North British days, Class A1 Pacific No 60162 St Johnstoun, looks *surprisingly unkempt*; this used to be one of Haymarket's most pristine 4-6-2s. It heads a stopping train to Edinburgh in the later 1950s, with the Gresley coaching stock in maroon.

Haymarket A3 Pacific No 60087 Blenheim awaits the right-away from Platform 3 with a Waverley route express in the 1950s.

In the early post-war years Holbeck Rebuilt Scot 4-6-0 No 6108 Seaforth Highlander *moves the northbound 'Thames-Clyde Express' out of Carlisle in the summer of 1947. The service was just regaining some respectability after wartime re-routeing and deceleration which had pathed it via Nottingham and Derby, extended its St Pancras–Glasgow itinerary by 44 miles and protracted its overall journey time to just over 11½ hours.*

A pre-war view of Carlisle's south end, when the overall roof still extended to the platform ends (compare with the facing picture, after some dismantling and substitution of low canopies). In those days Holbeck still had compound 4-4-0s and entrusted them with solo express work over Ais Gill, as is the case here with No 1068.

202

The three Southern Region diesel-electric 1Co-Co1s were switched to the West Coast main line in 1955 and for the next few years performed intermittently in multiple as well as singly on trains including the 'Royal Scot', alongside the LM twins Nos 10000/1. Tackling the up 'Royal Scot' on its own is the last and more powerful of the SR trio, the 2,000hp No 10203 built in 1954.

Between 1945 and 1950 the 'Royal Scot' was publicly non-stop between Euston and Glasgow all year round, the down train halting at Kingmoor, the up at Carlisle No 12 box for crew-change and examination. But in 1950 winter stops in Carlisle station were reinstated. Here the up train changes engines at the reversible No 3 platform: Polmadie Pacific No 46230 Duchess of Buccleuch, on the right, has just come off and is being replaced by one of the two post-war additions to the class, with detail variations. Note lack of fall-plate ahead of the cylinders, and electric lighting. No 46257 City of Salford, was a Camden Pacific.

BEATTOCK AND THE UPPER CLYDE VALLEY

The northbound ascent to Beattock summit was always the tougher of the two great West Coast main line climbs in the steam age. It was the longer grind, with 10 unbroken miles graded at nothing easier than 1 in 88, the last 5½ of them at an average of 1 in 75. That counselled a crew to keep speed well up for at least the first half of the bank, to the mid-point marked by the old Greskine box. Otherwise, particularly with a heavy Anglo-Scottish sleeper in tow on one of those characteristic mornings when a dank mist swirled round the hills, they could so easily stall before the top, unable to lengthen cut-off without the engine helplessly losing its feet. They had to watch water consumption more carefully than up Shap, too, because the Caledonian had been more thrifty in its spacing of water-troughs than the management south of the Border.

Anxiety at the rate she was gulping water – and the Stanier Duchesses were by common consent thirsty machines at the best of times – prompted a momentary relaxation of No 6234 *Duchess of Abercorn* during her stupendous assault of the hill with a 20-coach train of 610 tons gross on Sunday, 26 February 1939. Just out of Crewe works with double chimney and blastpipe modifications, the first of the type to be treated thus, No 6234 was being deliberately pressed to the limit on a special Crewe–Glasgow test (though the possibility of doubling up some trains north of Crewe for economy was the reason publicly advanced for putting No 6234 through the mill). So smoothly had she negotiated Shap, improving slightly on the 'Coronation Scot' streamliner's allowance from Carnforth to the summit, that the men in charge eschewed the stop provisionally tabled at Beattock station to take on water and, if thought prudent, a banker, and charged the foot of the climb at 60mph. With cut-off out to 40 per cent, the Duchess stormed the crest at a fraction under 30mph – would that the assuredly awesome sound had been recorded. Thereby she achieved the incredible feat, with such tonnage, of logging slightly less than even time for the 39.6 mostly uphill miles from Carlisle to the summit.

After only two hours' respite in Glasgow, since one objective of the test was to submit the Pacific to extreme load conditions within the limits of a normal roster, No 6234 was heading south with the same 20 coaches. In this direction she was set a timing of 116 minutes for the 102 miles to Carlisle and with the weather deteriorating into the makings of a blizzard it must have looked a tall order.

The southbound climb to the 1,014ft summit is not so taxing. The most trying stretch is the largely 1 in 102 between Motherwell and Law Junction. The gradients in the upper Clyde Valley are comparatively undemanding and the culminating five miles include a level interlude past Elvanfoot before the final two miles at 1 in 99 to the crest. Even so, with 610 tons – and, moreover, into the teeth of a snowstorm – it was hardly conceivable that the Duchess could dismiss the whole ascent from Symington at an average of 63.4mph and storm the 1 in 99 at a minimum of 62mph. But she did.

She made Carlisle no less than 9½ minutes ahead of the test schedule and in only 1½ minutes more than the contemporary allowance for the 'Coronation Scot', a train of half the weight. The streamliner could have been eclipsed had No 6234 been let rip down the southern slope of Beattock with as much abandon as sister engine No 46251 on a post-war 'Mid-day Scot' run once reported by O. S. Nock. A crew eager to recoup checks suffered before Carstairs assaulted the Lamington–Beattock Summit stretch at an average of 69.6mph with 13 on, then let *City of Nottingham* have its head to an unprecedented maximum of 105mph through Beattock station, so that the 10-mile descent was covered at an average of 91mph!

Unscheduled halt at Beattock summit to take water by Pacific No 46230 Duchess of Buccleuch on the up 'Royal Scot' of the early 1950s.

Though their Manchester–Glasgow train loads to no more than nine coaches, the crew of Carlisle Kingmoor Class 6 Pacific No 72009 *Clan Stewart* are playing safe and taking a banker from Beattock station.

Early 1950s Beattock banker in close-up at Harthope: ex-Caledonian 0-4-4T No 55187 helps the northbound 'Royal Scot'.

Facing page:
A memory of the morning Birmingham–Glasgow on the bank at Harthope, with Pacific No 46210 *Lady Patricia* making very heavy weather of a load likely to have exceeded 450 tons. The Birmingham–Glasgow was normally the second leg of a Polmadie shed lodging turn to Crewe that started with the up 'West Coast Postal'.

Overleaf:
Further up the bank, only 200 yards or so from the summit, the morning sun greets No 46223 *Princess Alice* on an overnight sleeper from Euston which includes a breakfast car, a luxury now almost forgotten. An ex-Caledonian 0-4-4T shoves manfully at the back.

Near the Clyde crossing at Lamington an unidentifiable Duchess makes a merry pace up the 1 in 300 with the morning Glasgow–Birmingham express, which features a through WR Hawksworth brake composite for Plymouth at the head of the formation.

Pacific No 46250 City of Lichfield speeds south through the upper Clyde Valley with the limited-load 'Caledonian'.